D1296114

"*The Risk of the Cross*, an intensely prayerful g
to Christians living in the nuclear age. Patterne
Mark's gospel, each chapter urges followers of
lives in pursuit of eradicating nuclear weapons. ⌐
urgent, Art Laffin helps us grapple with a reality stated bluntly by Plowshares
activist Steve Kelly, SJ: 'Nuclear weapons will not go away by themselves.'"

KATHY KELLY, *co-founder and co-coordinator of Voices for Creative Nonviolence*

"At a time when the Bulletin of the Atomic Scientists has moved the Doomsday
Clock to one hundred seconds before midnight, the faithful witness of the
Kings Bay Plowshares 7 and the publication of *The Risk of the Cross* offer
needed inspiration. This book should be widely shared."

MOLLY RUSH, *co-founder and retired director of the Thomas Merton Center, Pittsburgh,
Member of the Plowshares Eight*

"*The Risk of the Cross* impels readers to stand up and walk in the way of Christ's
nonviolent peace in this nuclear age. It helps us to find our vision of a nuclear-free world and seek it with grace and joy."

MARTHA HENNESSY, *participant in the Catholic Worker Movement and
Kings Bay Plowshares 7, granddaughter of Dorothy Day*

"*The Risk of the Cross* is an urgently needed and vitally important gospel guide
to help Catholics and all Christians more deeply understand the meaning
of Christian discipleship in a time of unprecedented global peril, and the
courageous action that is required to avert nuclear catastrophe and create a
nonviolent world."

MARTIN SHEEN

"The world is hungry for a paradigm shift toward nonviolence that alone can
move us beyond the false security of nuclear deterrence. *The Risk of the Cross*
is an excellent resource for courageous groups and individuals seeking to learn
about the danger presented by nuclear weapons, to pray and reflect together
on the scriptural call to just peace, and to act in response."

MARIE DENNIS, *senior advisor, co-president (2007–2019) Pax Christi International,
and editor,* Choosing Peace: The Catholic Church Returns to Gospel Nonviolence

"Truly, as Art Laffin observes in this profound, eloquent, and necessary book, there is a 'nuclear intention rooted in our hearts'—in our governments, in our budgets, in our foreign affairs, and too often in the lives of our churches as well. In 1981—when the prescient first edition of this book was published—the risk of the nuclear intention was palpable. Now, alas, it is less so; but it is Art Laffin's gift and his calling to make that intention palpable to us—and to suggest the ways we can oppose it by taking the risk of the cross."

Paul Elie, *Berkley Center for Religion, Peace, and World Affairs, Georgetown University, and author of* The Life You Save May Be Your Own: An American Pilgrimage

"The danger posed by nuclear weapons is not only a secular question; it poses a challenge to the heart of the Christian community. *The Risk of the Cross* takes the issue where it must be taken—into the local church. It continues to be a valuable resource that brings a strong biblical and church teaching to bear on what is still the greatest threat to the human race."

Jim Wallis, *president and founder of* Sojourners

"Let this book dare you to live with a renewed confidence and faith. Those of us who follow the Prince of Peace must have as much courage, ingenuity, and imagination as those who believe in war. Here is an invitation to explore the narrow way that leads to life, in a world that continues to take the broad road that leads to destruction."

Shane Claiborne, *author, activist, co-founder of* The Simple Way and Red Letter Christians

"Studied in community, pondered, attended to, Mark's gospel led to this book. *The Risk of the Cross* unsheathes the sword of the Spirit which both wounds and heals. It allows St. Mark to speak for himself, to speak for Jesus, to judge the church. This is the wisdom of the authors—not to get in the way of the Author, just as Mark allows us to hear from Jesus: starkly, simply, luminously."

Daniel Berrigan, SJ, *for first edition of* The Risk of the Cross
(Daniel Berrigan died in 2016)

NEW EDITION

FOREWORDS BY
HENRI J. M. NOUWEN *and* **JOHN DEAR**

The
Risk
OF THE
Cross

LIVING GOSPEL NONVIOLENCE
IN THE NUCLEAR AGE

Arthur Laffin

TWENTY-THIRD
PUBLICATIONS
twentythirdpublications.com

TWENTY-THIRD PUBLICATIONS
One Montauk Avenue, Suite 200
New London, CT 06320
(860) 437-3012 or (800) 321-0411
www.twentythirdpublications.com

ISBN: 978-1-62785-540-2
Printed in the U.S.A.

A division of Bayard, Inc.

Contents

ACKNOWLEDGMENTS

I am immensely grateful to many people for their prayerful support and encouragement in the publication of this new edition of *The Risk of the Cross*. I first want to acknowledge those who brought the first edition of this book to fruition. Without them this new volume would not be possible. Dating back to 1979, Fr. Ed Nadolny offered his wholehearted support for this project and was primarily responsible for publishing "The Call to Faithfulness: The Arms Race and the Gospel of Mark." This study guide was later revised and became *The Risk of the Cross*. I am forever grateful to my original co-authors, the late Chris Grannis, who died in 2007, and Elin Schade. Elin is now semi-retired and has given her wholehearted support for this new edition.

I am very thankful to Dean Hammer for his significant input in the original book and for making the initial contact with Seabury Press, who would publish it. During the preparation of the first edition, Henri Nouwen provided crucial spiritual guidance to Chris, Elin, and myself, helping us to deepen our understanding of Christian discipleship and the healing power of the Eucharist.

I want to convey my sincere thanks to Marie Dennis, former co-president of Pax Christi International (PCI), and Nick Mele, of the PCI Washington, DC, Working Group. Following a meeting to discuss how to encourage the Church to become more active in promoting nuclear abolition and gospel nonviolence, they were strongly supportive of my suggestion to update *The Risk of the Cross* and use it as an educational resource toward that end. I am extremely thankful to PCI and Pax Christi USA for their special support in helping this book to be published and in promoting its use.

Through God's amazing grace, Twenty-Third Publications accepted this new edition. I am so deeply thankful to Kathy Hendricks, Therese Ratliff, Dan Connors, and the Twenty-Third Publications team for believing in the importance of this book and for all they did to assist in its publication.

Nick and Mary Mele, spent long hours working on this manuscript; Amanda Muir helped greatly with typing and proofreading the manuscript.

I am extremely grateful to Stephen Kobasa for his superb editing help. Their efforts to prepare this book for publication have been invaluable.

I am deeply grateful to John Dear for his input and encouragement for this book, for writing a new foreword, and his tireless work in proclaiming the gospel of nonviolence.

I also want to convey great appreciation to all the people whose contributions appear in the appendix sections of this book.

I want to express heartfelt gratitude to my wife, Colleen McCarthy, for her steadfast support throughout this entire project. I am also most grateful to my son, Carlos, and for the prayers and support I have received from my extended family.

I am especially thankful, too, to my community of the Dorothy Day Catholic Worker for their enduring support. I am also indebted to many friends from Jonah House, Atlantic Life Community, Southern Life Community, Pacific Life Community, the extended Plowshares community, the wider Catholic Worker movement, Voices for Creative Nonviolence, Pax Christi, Journey of Hope, Witness Against Torture, TASSC, Little Friends for Peace, Assisi Community, Sojourners, Pace e Bene, Caldwell Chapel Community, 8th Day Faith Community, Weston Priory, St. Al's, Holy Redeemer, St. Teresa of Avila, St. Gabriel, and Our Lady Queen of Peace parishes, Community of Sant'Egidio, and different communities of faith and nonviolent resistance around the United States and abroad that I have had the great opportunity to be associated with during these last four decades. I have learned so much from them about the true meaning of radical Christian discipleship.

Finally, I want to dedicate this book to the Hibakusha who ceaselessly appeal for worldwide nuclear abolition; to all the nameless victims who have suffered and died because of empire, war, and racial violence; to all who have labored and risked their freedom to create a nonviolent disarmed world; and to all who have inspired me in my journey of discipleship and peacemaking, including all peace-and-justice-makers-past who are present now among the holy cloud of witnesses and who have shown the world how to be a witness to Jesus' way of nonviolence and create the Beloved Community.

Arthur Laffin
March 2020

FOREWORD TO
THE FIRST EDITION

Is there hope for history? This question, which was hardly asked in the fifties, has become an agonizing question for many in the eighties. The source of this anxiety is no longer just our individual or communal mortality but the death of all of history. Slowly a new consciousness is developing, a consciousness that has to come to terms with the possibility that history can come to an end.

It is this new consciousness that led Elin Schade, Chris Grannis, and Art Laffin to reflect on the meaning of discipleship in our nuclear age. They realized that because collective suicide is a possibility, Christian discipleship has entered into a decisively new phase. To follow Christ on the way of the cross, to leave father, mother, brother, and sister for his sake, and to lay down your life for your friends—these are challenges with a truly new meaning when the future itself has become doubtful.

Elin, Chris, and Art are not just three authors who decided to write a book together on one of the burning issues of our time. No, they are a woman and two men who have dedicated their lives to offering hope to history by all they do, say, and think. It has been a very great privilege for me to know them during the years in which they laid the foundation for this book. What has most impressed me is the movement in their lives from protest to prayer. The many protest actions in which they participated in the past made them realize with growing clarity that only a deep spiritual rootedness in the living Word of God would allow them to continue to say *No* to the escalating nuclear arms race without losing their own mental and spiritual integrity.

Slowly they came to realize that the value of their protest was based less on their ability to change the course of political history than on their vocation to announce the hope of the cross in the midst of a self-destructive human society. They came to see that the good news of the gospel is that Jesus Christ has overcome not only our personal deaths but also the death of human history. They came to understand that the challenge of the gospel is to offer hope in all places and at all times, and that their different actions for peace would be fruitful only when they are nurtured by this hope. The hope of the gospel is something other than the optimistic expectation that things will be better within a few decades, something other than the wish that politicians will change their minds, something other even than the desire to prevent the world from being destroyed by human hands. The hope of the gospel is based on the spiritual knowledge that love is stronger than death.

In this book Elin, Chris, and Art offer the best of their most personal discoveries that they made during their struggle to find an honest as well as fearless response to the threat of a nuclear holocaust. In the Gospel of Mark they found a spirituality which enables them to be joyful even when the political situation looks quite grim, to be peaceful even when the sounds of war are all around us, and to be hopeful even when many people show signs of true despair. But they do more than just present the fruits of their own life in community. They also offer their ideas in such a way that those who explore them can find a new community themselves. Thus, this book, which comes out of a life together, is also a book that leads to a new life together. It is therefore a truly Christian book. This becomes very clear when the authors point to the Eucharist as the basis and source of community in the midst of a chaotic fear-ridden world.

I am heartened by this book, heartened too by the way it was written, and deeply grateful for the hope it offers not just to individual people but to history as well.

Henri J.M. Nouwen
1981

FOREWORD TO
THE REVISED EDITION

Not long ago, a friend and I attended a rally for "Fire Drill Fridays" in front of the US Capitol in Washington, DC. Actor Jane Fonda led nearly one thousand of us in a rally for climate justice, followed by a march to the Hart Senate Office Building where she joined 140 of us who were arrested in nonviolent civil disobedience for sitting in and demanding an end to fossil fuel development and environmental destruction.

While standing on the US Capitol lawn, getting ready for the civil disobedience, my friend Michele Dunne, a colleague of mine at Pace e Bene, asked me about the church's teaching on suffering. "I never understood that phrase, 'Offer it up,'" she said. We had been listening to passionate speeches against war, injustice, and environmental destruction, so I answered. "Well, for the record, Jesus never said that." Michele looked at me quizzically.

"What Jesus actually said, over and over again, was, 'If you want to be my follower, you have to take up the cross and follow me.' So, the real question is, 'What does it mean to take up the cross? What does the cross of Jesus mean for us today?'"

I looked around, pointed to the crowd in front of the US Capitol as it lined up to march and engage in nonviolent civil disobedience, and said, "This is the cross of Jesus."

Then I told her about a shocking statement made by a theologian in the 1960s which I've never forgotten. The cross is not having a difficult job, a difficult boss, a difficult in-law, or a flat tire, he wrote. The cross is not having a bad day and lamenting, "I'm carrying my cross."

Two thousand years ago, the cross was state-sanctioned execution of revolutionaries by the empire. Crucifixion was punishment for rocking the boat, for disturbing the peace. So, when the evangelists speak of "carrying the cross" as a requirement of following Jesus, they mean we have to live in daily nonviolent resistance to the empire, to the entire culture of violence, come what may. This is the normal, ordinary life of the Christian.

Carrying the cross means speaking out and taking public nonviolent action against the systems of death that are killing so many millions around the US and the world. It means taking a strong nonviolent public stand against war, racism, poverty, hunger, nuclear weapons, and environmental destruction, and building a grassroots movement of nonviolence to resist and transform that culture of violence into something we have never known, an entirely new culture of nonviolence. And it means, for the evangelists, doing it in the same meticulous spirit of nonviolence that Jesus practiced, so that we accept nonviolently the consequences of our actions.

From this perspective, those who carried the cross during their lives were people like the Abolitionists, who worked nonviolently to end slavery; the Civil Rights movement activists, who worked to end segregation; and the young students today working to end gun violence and environmental destruction.

The key revelation of the gospels, according to Mahatma Gandhi and Rev. Dr. Martin Luther King Jr., is that Jesus was totally nonviolent, that he taught meticulous nonviolence, and that he formed and led a grassroots campaign of nonviolence from Galilee to Jerusalem, where he confronted the ruling authorities in an act of civil disobedience in the temple and was subsequently arrested, tried, tortured, and executed. He was not killed in a random act of violence. He was killed for building a nonviolent movement, for opposing the empire, for talking about "the Kingdom of God," a whole new culture of nonviolence. His was a revolutionary, prophetic nonviolence that was a threat to the empire.

Note that from this perspective, the Eucharist is a new covenant of nonviolence. If he were a military general, he would have said, "Go break their bodies for me. Go shed their blood for me." Instead, in the Eucharist, we are invited to share his way of nonviolence: "My body broken for you. My blood shed for you. Do this!" Note, too, the last thing his community heard him say before he died, his last words to the Church: there, in the Garden of Gethsemane, about to be arrested, he said: "Put down the sword." Shocked by the realization that he's serious about nonviolence, that he's not going to defend himself with violence, they all run away. Jesus is taken off and killed by the empire.

But the story doesn't end there. The gospels report that he rose from the dead, in the same spirit of peaceful nonviolence, and encouraged his disciples to carry on his campaign of nonviolence, which they did. The early Church was a grassroots movement of nonviolence by disciples of the nonviolent Jesus. In these terrible times, many of us are trying to reclaim that holy tradition of active nonviolence, what the gospel calls "carrying the cross." That's what Art Laffin and his friends proposed nearly forty years ago when this book was first published.

I remember meeting Art just as the book came out. It was important to many of us because he used the language of the cross to help us understand our discipleship to the nonviolent Jesus and therefore our public actions, including civil disobedience, against war, injustice, and nuclear weapons. Like our friend Henri Nouwen, I was heartened by this book.

Nearly forty years later, this new revised version is still greatly needed, because few talk about the cross as a way to understand our discipleship, as a way to understand our movement work for justice and disarmament. This guidebook can help us reflect on the gospel of Jesus and what it means to follow him—by practicing his meticulous nonviolence and carrying the cross through lifelong nonviolent resistance to the culture of violence, war, and environmental destruction.

The times are so dangerous. With systemic injustice trapping billions in extreme poverty, and with governmental corruption, unparalleled corporate greed, systemic racism, the rise of fascism, and permanent warfare, we face a global epidemic of violence. But actually, we are closer to nuclear war than ever. And with catastrophic climate change, we now face the real possibility of global destruction, the likes of which the world has never seen.

The only antidote to the global epidemic of violence that threatens us all is a global, grassroots, people-power movement of nonviolence for disarmament, justice, and care of creation, the likes of which the world has never seen. This is what Jesus started long ago. We Christians need to be part of these grassroots movements of nonviolence, not only to help protect humanity and creation, but to help us follow the nonviolent Jesus. As Christians, we carry the cross by standing up, stepping forward, taking action, and speaking out publicly against every aspect of the culture of violence and war, but particularly against nuclear weapons and environmental destruction. We follow Jesus on the way to global nonviolent transformation by risking the cross in our daily lives, that is, by sharing in his Paschal Mystery.

This new edition comes to print just as we mark the seventy-fifth anniversaries of the US atomic bombings of Hiroshima and Nagasaki. Through this book, we are guided to become more mature disciples of the nonviolent Jesus and to do our part with the global grassroots movement of nonviolence so that Jesus' global campaign of nonviolence can make new inroads, so that one day, in fact, we will end our wars and abolish nuclear weapons, as well as poverty, racism, and the death penalty; we will protect creation once and for all and welcome Jesus' reign of peace on earth.

On that day, we will realize the wisdom of the cross and be glad we took the risk. On that day, we will welcome the nonviolent Jesus' resurrection gift of peace and enter a new culture of nonviolence.

May this book give you courage to study the gospel all over again from the perspective of Gandhian/Kingian nonviolence and to take another step forward in the footsteps of the nonviolent Jesus on the way of the cross, the path of nonviolent resistance to systemic injustice and war. Together, may we risk the cross, practice resurrection, and welcome a whole new world of nonviolence. Amen.

John Dear
March 2020

INTRODUCTION TO
THE FIRST EDITION AND
HOW TO USE THIS BOOK

Jesus tells us, "Fear is useless; what is needed is trust" (5:36). These words from Mark's gospel capture the spirit we wish to bear witness to in our lives and to express in this book. We have been called together by a faith in the power of God, which is manifested in weakness—our own and that of others like us who struggle to confront the violent despair of the nuclear threat with a message of Christian hope.

This book is the fruit of the Kingdom of God mysteriously at work in our midst. We, the writers, come from communities of faith nourished by the word of God and the Eucharist. In our prayer together, we have been deeply stirred by the vulnerable, forgiving love of Jesus powerfully expressed on the cross. His nonviolent example in the face of the consummate evil and blatant injustices of his day informs our struggles as his twentieth-century disciples. As people striving to follow his way, we reject all weapons of war—both conventional and nuclear—as being diametrically opposed to Christ's Kingdom and his way of salvation through willing self-sacrifice.

One of our primary goals in writing the discussion articles is to discover, and to help others discover, the contemporary meaning of discipleship. In contrast to the other evangelists, Mark portrays the disciples in a largely critical light. They appear sincere but misguided; they struggle for power among themselves and resist Christ's message of the cross. Thus, Mark's presentation of discipleship—a central theme of his gospel—is a study about struggle and human failure, not a study of heroic, faithful obedience. Mark's description of the disciples' failure lends itself well to an honest examination of our own faith and moral attitudes. In view of the generally unquestioning consent Christians give to nuclear weapons, Mark's exposition of the meaning of true discipleship strongly recommends itself.

Mark uses a literary technique that reinforces the contrast between true and false discipleship. He frames or juxtaposes various accounts of Jesus' healing, teaching, and feeding—the range of his life-promoting actions—with contrasting accounts of behavior by others that are life-denying. For example, the healing of the two blind men before and after Jesus' three predictions of his death and resurrection highlights the spiritual blindness of the disciples, who are incapable of comprehending the real significance of these predictions. The first four sessions in the book are organized around particular Markan frames. We have adopted Mark's framing technique as our own and have extended it to the contemporary situation, framing, with the example of Jesus' life and teaching, questions concerning the buildup of nuclear weapons.

We have tried to stay close to this gospel, to imitate Mark's evocative yet compact style. And as much as possible we have avoided both theological and political concepts that would distract the reader from the central questions of discipleship.

We write as Americans about an urgent issue facing our society, but it is the quality of the human problem, not the national one, that we wish to examine. Our concern is global and encompasses the whole human family. We confront not merely the American or Russian mentality, its weapons and technology, but, more important, the human fear and moral failure that are universal and that lie beneath all motives of violence.

What distinguishes this work, we believe, from others that treat the problem of nuclear weapons in a gospel context is our effort to interrelate the question of conscience with the question of faith. We are not just presenting an ethical argument on pacifism in the nuclear age; we are inviting as well a leap of faith, the intimate moment of repentance and conversion.

Such a moment flows from a pattern of human experience that is described throughout Mark's gospel—the pattern of perceiving and responding to the authority of Christ. The perception theme developed in the earlier sessions moves from the initial question of "Who is Jesus?" to the problem of discipleship as the journey to the cross, and then to the contemporary problem of blindness to the full implications of nuclear weapons. The later sessions treat the faith and moral responses respectively, while the final gathering—in liturgy—celebrates the response of hope. This liturgy of the Word and Eucharist (session 5) culminates the search and reflection process of the previous four sessions and inaugurates a new commitment to faith and struggle. Prayer and community are integral aspects of the Christian life. Sharing prayer establishes community; building community is itself a prayer. Both aspects together enable dynamic growth, a process based on relationships of trust. This book has grown out of such a process and, we hope, will help others to grow and yield fruit if used in the same way. We encourage a careful, contemplative attitude of prayer during the course of the sessions as well as an open, sensitive sharing among the members of the group. The questions of faith that are posed do not lend themselves to easy or immediate answers. A genuine trust in the Spirit and in one another is needed in order to face these questions honestly and to enable moments of repentance and conversion.

Suggestions for group use
While the book may be used for individual reflection—and we encourage that!—the overall format is designed to assist both new and established prayer and gospel-study groups. For new groups, we recommend an initial gathering, perhaps for a meal and personal introduction, before undertaking the first session together.

The basic gospel-study section consists of five sessions. Ideally, these would be scheduled on a consecutive weekly basis. The length of each session can vary from one and one-half to three hours depending on the needs or limitations of the group. The first four sessions consist of the following elements with suggested time allotments for a two-hour session:

Session Elements	Suggested Time Allotment
Opening Prayer	10 MINUTES
Reading from Mark, Review of the Articles	20 MINUTES
Discussion of Questions	1 HOUR
Evaluation and Planning	15 MINUTES
Closing Prayer	15 MINUTES

We encourage the designation of a facilitator for each session to ensure a smooth and fair process, and we recommend that this role be shared or rotated among the members of the group. The facilitator is expected to invite introductions when necessary, to arrange for the opening prayer and the reading aloud of the Mark passage, to focus and moderate the group discussion, and to keep track of the time. Each participant, of course, shares responsibility for maintaining a focused and productive discussion and reflection.

The material provided for each session should be prepared before the gathering. The opening prayer and the Mark reading should be read aloud clearly and very slowly by someone familiar with the text. Silence is an important complement to these reflective readings.

For a fruitful discussion we recommend that the articles for discussion be read at least twice and the discussion questions be prepared before the session gathering. A twenty-minute review period during each session is suggested.

Allowing time at the close of each session for some group evaluation and planning is an important way of examining the process and dynamics within the group, of accounting for needs met or unmet, and of ensuring an adequate preparation for the next session.

The prayer closing each session begins with reflection on verses selected from the Mark reading. This can be followed by a period of spontaneous personal prayer and can conclude with a song or prayer familiar to all. This occasion should not be slighted because of time considerations. Again, we affirm the importance of prayer within the group experience—its virtue in enabling growth cannot be underestimated.

The appendices of this book serve as a very important supplement to each of the five sessions. They contain a wide range of historical, political, and economic data on nuclear weapons. The appendices also include religious and moral statements on peace and nuclear disarmament issued by groups and individuals, ways in which churches and Christian groups can become more active peacemakers, a list of groups working on national and local levels for justice and peace, and lists of books and films [and websites]. The appendix section is organized for use concurrently with the discussion articles and discussion questions. Each corresponding appendix should be read by the group prior to the session gathering. Appendix 1, "The Courage to Start" by Robert Aldridge, should be read in preparation for the first session.

Christopher Grannis,
Arthur Laffin, and
Elin Schade
October 1980

INTRODUCTION TO
THE REVISED EDITION

It has been 39 years since I contributed to writing the first edition of *The Risk of the Cross*, a project that evolved out of an earlier work written primarily for Catholics in Connecticut and published as a study guide for church use in 1979. Using central themes of Mark's gospel, *The Risk of the Cross*, which was published two years later, was written with the hope that followers of Jesus, in the context of a prayerful community, would better understand the meaning of Christian discipleship in the Nuclear Age. The book was well received, widely used by church groups across the US, and went into five printings.

Today, as in 1981, there is a great need for Christians, in light of their faith, to address the nuclear threat that imperils all life and to actively become Jesus' peace and justice makers. Today, in this time of perpetual war, there is also an equally important need to address and act on the related threat of climate and environmental devastation, which endangers all of creation. While this book is focused exclusively on the gospel response to the nuclear threat, I hope that the reader will keep in mind how this gospel study of the nuclear danger can also apply to the climate crisis.

As I write, another global crisis—the coronavirus (COVID-19) outbreak—has emerged, causing widespread illness, numerous deaths, and impacting every facet of daily life. Public officials have issued stay at home and social distancing measures, schools and churches are closed. For Jesus' followers, the gospel dictates our faith response to every challenge we face, including this pandemic. Jesus instructs us that faith is the antidote to fear, to trust in God, and to love our neighbor. Thus, our faith in Jesus compels us to stand for life wherever it is threatened, care for those in need, and act for justice. As we find creative ways to put our faith into responsible action regarding this crisis, we must demand that political officials redirect all funding for nuclear war preparations and from an exorbitant US military budget ($738 billion in 2020) to meet urgent public health needs, to safeguard "essential" workers, and to protect and provide comprehensive testing and assistance for those most at risk—communities of color, the poor, elderly, uninsured, unemployed, homeless, prisoners, and undocumented. This theft of the public treasury for warfare instead of health care is a sin and crime!

The COVID-19 pandemic has exposed many critical problems facing our society and world, but also countless acts of goodness, especially those of health-care workers and frontline workers. It has also helped many to recognize that to sufficiently understand its origin, treat, contain, and, ultimately, end it will require mutual cooperation by governments and people worldwide. Still, as the world struggles to cope with this pandemic and an uncertain future, the nuclear threat remains an ever-present danger. The pandemic serves as an ominous warning of the unimaginable reality that would ensue should there ever be a nuclear war. Consider the global effects of a nuclear war: annihilation of total societies, untold casualties, a cancer pandemic caused by nuclear radiation, widespread famine, nuclear winter, and an uninhabitable earth. The primary intent of this book is to encourage every conceivable effort to avert such a global catastrophe.

It was truly a gift and blessing to co-author the original edition of this book with Elin Schade and Chris Grannis. Henri Nouwen, who wrote the foreword, provided invaluable support for our joint efforts. Since its publication, Chris and Henri, both dear friends and exemplary followers of Jesus, have gone home to God. Now among the holy cloud of witnesses, they continue to inspire many others and me. Their faith-filled and loving spirit, along with that of Elin's, reflected in the discussion articles and foreword of the book, carries over into this new edition and graces its pages.

The original introduction to *The Risk of the Cross* provides a detailed explanation of the purpose and content of the book. In this edition it is important to make note of some new changes. The discussion articles in this new edition are primarily based on the original edition. However, these articles required some revisions in certain places for editorial reasons and in order to provide important new insights from more recently published biblical commentaries. The reader should know that the intention of the discussion articles is not to offer an intensive exegetical examination of Mark's gospel but rather to ascertain how the gospel calls us to be faithful disciples in a time of unprecedented peril.

The appendix sections contain many new pieces and have been updated to give the reader important current information about the nuclear issue.

Since *The Risk of the Cross* was first published, Ched Myers published a groundbreaking book on Mark's gospel: *Binding the Strong Man: A Political Reading of Mark's Story of Jesus.* This is the first commentary on the Gospel of Mark to systematically apply a multidisciplinary approach, called "socio-literary method." Myers integrates literary criticism, sociohistorical exegesis, and political hermeneutics in his investigation of Mark—the oldest story of Jesus—as a "manifesto of radical discipleship." In my view, this is the definitive book on Mark's gospel. I strongly recommend it as a companion resource to this new edition.

There are many invaluable insights from *Binding the Strongman* that have been very helpful to my interpretation of what the gospel writer Mark is trying to convey in his narrative of Jesus. One insight includes applying the following guidelines on how best to read and interpret a gospel passage: develop a narrative structure analysis of a gospel account; identify the plot and outline of the story; identify the setting; identify the characters; and develop a theme and conclusion.

Another key insight involves a recognition of two central themes that are in the background throughout reading Mark's gospel: "repentance" and "resistance." Living under the brutal occupation of the Roman Empire, Jesus declared: "The kingdom of God is at hand. Repent and believe in the gospel"(Mark 1:15). This repentance implies not only a conversion of heart but a turning away from empire. Jesus then calls his disciples to follow him, to proclaim the reign of God, and to nonviolently resist the forces of evil and death. Living in the US, an empire responsible for so much needless death and suffering in our world today, we need to heed Jesus' proclamation now more than ever.

In preparation for this new edition, I thought back to 1981, the year that this book was first published. The nuclear threat was as palpable and imminent then as it is today. There was open talk by government officials of a nuclear exchange between the United States and the Soviet Union. Then, the Bulletin of the Atomic Scientists turned its "Doomsday Clock" to three minutes before midnight. Three years later, it was changed to a mere one minute before.

Today, due to the existential dangers of nuclear war and climate change—that are compounded by cyber-enabled information warfare, undercutting society's ability to respond—the erosion of the international political infrastructure to manage these threats, upgrades to existing nuclear systems, and worsening world tensions, the "Doomsday Clock" is set to 100 seconds before midnight.

Other recent developments have further exacerbated the nuclear peril. Russia and the US possess an estimated combined total of over 12,600 nuclear weapons, many of which are on hair-trigger alert. Both countries are also developing hypersonic weapons that could become nuclear capable. US and NATO missile defense systems ring Russia and China, increasing already heightened tensions. A new US space force has been created to oversee military control and domination of space. The US is committed to a thirty-year upgrade of its nuclear arsenal at an estimated cost of $1.7 trillion.

Additionally, the current US administration has threatened to use nuclear weapons against adversaries on several occasions. During this past year, the US withdrew from the Iran Nuclear Deal and the INF Treaty with Russia and carried out a subcritical nuclear test, a flagrant violation of the Comprehensive Nuclear Test Ban Treaty. And Pentagon policy makers have declared that a limited nuclear war could be waged and won, according to the new *Doctrine for Joint Nuclear Operations*. This doctrine is the latest manifestation of a long-held existing Pentagon policy positing that the US must be prepared at all times to use whatever military force is necessary, including the use of nuclear weapons, to protect its vital strategic and geopolitical interests in the world. The deployment in February 2020 of the "lower-yield" W76-2 nuclear warhead on Trident missiles, a smaller warhead the military believes is more usable, increases the risk of nuclear war.

Although humanity still remains on the brink of nuclear catastrophe, there have been compelling and courageous disarmament actions and initiatives by grassroots groups, plowshares activists, and peacemakers worldwide, papal pronouncements condemning the mere possession of nuclear weapons, NGOs like the International Campaign to Abolish Nuclear Weapons (ICAN), and the historic UN Treaty on the Prohibition of Nuclear Weapons. Also to commemorate the seventy-fifth anniversary of the US nuclear bombings of Hiroshima and Nagasaki on August 6–9, 2020, there will be numerous international actions calling for nuclear abolition. These are all signs of great encouragement and hope.

I am deeply grateful to Nick and Mary Mele, who have worked tirelessly on this book. Without their efforts it would not be possible to publish this new edition. Together, we hope that this new edition of *The Risk of the Cross* will help Catholics and all Christians to better grasp the absolute threat that nuclear weapons pose to all God's Creation and lead people to take nonviolent action to bring about a disarmed world. Moreover, we pray it will help Christians realize that to follow Jesus' way of the cross today requires that we nonviolently resist empire, systemic oppression, and all forms of violence.

The Hibakusha (A-Bomb Survivors) plead to the world: "Humanity and nuclear weapons cannot coexist." Martin Luther King Jr. exhorts us: "The choice today is…either nonviolence or non-existence." And Pope Francis declares: "The total elimination of nuclear weapons is both a challenge and a moral and humanitarian imperative of our time."

The crises of our time reveal how broken and unsustainable the established order is and present an opportunity for a global paradigm shift toward a more just, sustainable, and peaceful world. We can no longer accept as "normal" those established institutions and structures founded on racism, greed, oppression, violence, and injustice that are destroying humanity and the planet. Now is the time to act in solidarity with people worldwide working for nonviolent social transformation. Dr. King proclaimed: "Our only hope today lies in our ability to recapture the revolutionary spirit and go out into a sometimes hostile world declaring eternal hostility to poverty, racism and militarism." If the human family and Earth, our common home, are to survive, if the children are to have a future, we need to recapture the hope and revolutionary spirit that Dr. King speaks of and reject empire; abolish war, nuclear weapons, killer drones, biological and chemical weapons, and all weapons; end environmental devastation; and eradicate systemic racism, inequality, and poverty. Moreover, we need to commit our lives to the commandment of gospel nonviolence as we join with others seeking to create the Beloved Community, thereby making God's reign of love, peace, and justice a reality for our world. For with God all things are possible (Mark 10:27)!

Arthur Laffin
March 2020

Who is Jesus?

OPENING PRAYER

Lord Jesus, we gather in your name to be healed and taught by you. In a world marred by manifest evils—starvation, poverty, war, disease, prejudice, crime, and the violence of lethal armaments—we recognize you as the One who can forgive our sins. You know our human condition, the often-contradictory longings of our hearts, and the powerlessness we feel in the face of such complex and pervasive evil. You know us as both victim and perpetrator, and still you offer us your healing and intimacy. We rejoice that you "have come for sinners, not the self-righteous," because we know our need for you. Extend your reign in our hearts, teach us divine standards of judging and acting, and help us become new vessels of your Spirit. Empower us to resist all the forces of death that we and our society are bound by and to usher in your reign of justice, love, and peace. We ask this for the glory of your name. Amen.

GOSPEL READING

Mark 2:1—3:6; 3:22–27

DISCUSSION ARTICLE ✠ *Who is Jesus?*

In Mark's gospel, Jesus breaks onto the stage of history, his way prepared by the Baptist's resounding cry in the wilderness: "One more powerful than I is to come after me. I am not fit to stoop and untie his sandal straps. I have baptized you with water; he will baptize you with the Holy Spirit" (1:7–8).

Who is this Jesus, this more powerful One, who will baptize with the

Holy Spirit? These identity questions are pivotal to the message of Mark and crucial to the proper engagement of the reader in the journey of faith that the gospel envisions. The gospels are faith proclamations—not mere biographies—and as such they aim to elicit a faith response from the reader. For Mark, the faith response becomes an incarnation of trust, the fruit of a deep personal relationship. The central question of faith is: In whom do I trust? Not: What do I believe?

At the turning point of Mark's gospel, just as at the turning point of our lives, Jesus asks his would-be disciples two critical questions concerning his identity: "Who do people say that I am?" and, more important, "And *you*, who do *you* say that I am?" (8:27, 29). Like Peter, we must be able to answer personally. It is not enough to recite time-honored confessions, nor merely to mouth popular piety (8:27, 28). Jesus wants more than "lip service" and "empty reverence" (7:6). He searches our hearts for the childlike trust in his guidance that will enable us to journey with him to the fulfillment of the Christian mission—a way that leads to the life-giving sacrifice of the cross.

An authentic response to the question "Who is Jesus?" sets in motion a process of conversion that becomes a journey of faith and discipleship. The keener and truer our perceptions of Jesus' identity, the more radical our following him becomes. As we allow ourselves to be drawn further into the mystery of his person, our understanding and responsibility deepen proportionally. Discipleship becomes an imperative of faith; as a result, we take the pattern of Jesus' life and death as our own. We learn that Jesus' way leads to the cross but that, contrary to expectation, the cross represents not defeat and destruction but victory and healing. This gospel paradox, namely, that the way to preserve one's life is to lose it for the sake of Christ and the gospel (8:35), stands as the touchstone of true Christian fidelity.

The journey of faith begins at the Lord's invitation; he finds us in our places of marginal existence—in our personal Galilees—where we hunger for good news and the promise of liberation. There, the Lord announces a healing proclamation: "This is the time of fulfillment! The reign of God is at hand! Reform your lives and believe in the gospel!" (1:15). Our lives, our ways of seeing, judging, and acting are transformed by Christ as we experience his reign in our midst. We need to give ourselves over to the process of conversion and to be taught the path of discipleship. We are called to journey from the place of initial encounter with the life-giving words and healing touch of Christ to the fullness of communion with his life and mission, cross, and resurrection. As disciples, we trace Christ's steps from the marginal places where hope first ignites, through the deepening of faith, to the test of love. Following Jesus, we gradually come to appreciate that the journey of discipleship leads inexorably to the cross and beyond the empty tomb to fuller life and renewed mission.

Conflict of authorities: divine or human

For contemporary believers, the *authority* of Jesus rests on his *identity* as the Christ and the Son of God; indeed, it is with just these titles that Mark introduces Jesus (1:1). For the first disciples, however, the opposite was true; they came to know Jesus' *identity* by first experiencing his *authority*.

Mark records the earliest reaction to Jesus thus: "The people were spellbound by his teaching because he taught with authority and not like the scribes....All who looked on were amazed. They began to ask one another: What does this mean? A completely new teaching in a spirit of authority. He gives orders to unclean spirits and they obey him!" (1:22, 27). From the beginning people sense a power and authority in Jesus they had not known before in their religious leaders. Jesus is different. His words authoritatively proclaim "a completely new teaching" and his actions convey the divine energies of mercy and compassion. People begin to wonder deeply: Who is this Jesus?

For each person in the gospel who responds to the revelation of Jesus' identity with awe and expectancy, another recoils with indignation at the presumption of his claims. To some, Jesus is the longed-for liberator; to others, he is a rank blasphemer and an insidious threat to orthodoxy. In either case, Jesus demands attention. One's perception of Jesus determines the nature of one's response; lines of allegiance and enmity form early and intensify with time. Mark carefully charts people's various perceptions of Jesus and their diverse reactions to him. We, reading the gospel today, respond to Jesus with the same diversity, and so it becomes our story as well. We are invited to enter into the Spirit's dynamic, which calls disciples in every age. The critical issues then become: What is my perception of Jesus? and What will be my response?

As early as chapter 2, the radical nature of Christ's claims begins to make its impact, and consequently, his authority is challenged by the guardians of the status quo. After sketching a typical day in the life of Jesus, Mark presents five rapid scenes depicting him in conflict with various opponents (2:1—3:6). Jesus' authority becomes the critical focus of each incident; each time his opponents ask more stridently: Why does he act in this way? What gives him the *right* to "violate" sacred traditions and ancient religious practices? These questions put to any other person would be legitimate, but because they are put to Jesus, there can be no satisfactory answer unless the questioner possesses a receptive faith. Jesus, as the decisive agent of God's Kingdom, is the Lord who rightly determines what is sacred or profane.

All five conflicts, by their imagery and content, enrich our understanding of Jesus' identity and at the same time disclose God's plan of salvation in Christ. In each incident, Jesus reveals divine values and priorities by word and deed. Conflict occurs when these divine standards—namely, mercy and compassion—clash with the stone-cold dictates of tradition or self-righteous piety. Jesus offers sinners fullness of life and divine intimacy, and his opponents resent him for it. Jesus requires conversion from his followers, but these opponents stand arrogantly secure in their knowledge of the law and the prophets. Their self-righteousness blinds them to Jesus and to the limitless compassion of the God he mediates. They refuse to abandon their constricting notions of God; with their paralyzed faith and withered love, they become countersigns to the healing Jesus has come to offer. The humble, the receptive, and the broken are healed physically and spiritually, while the proud and the complacent harden their hearts and close their minds (3:5). The contrast of responses is instructive for all disciples.

The paralytic and the man with the withered hand

The arrival of the paralytic carried to Jesus by his friends serves as the occasion for Christ to address a more crippling malady, the paralysis of spirit that arises out of sin and hardness of heart. Heedless of public ridicule and censure, four faith-filled friends of a paralyzed man tear open the roof over Jesus in order to lower their companion into his presence. Such faith and childlike trustfulness cannot go unrewarded; it is just this suppleness of spirit that Jesus is looking for and works wonders with. Jesus forgives the man his sins!

We may be disappointed with this solution to the man's dilemma. We wonder why at first Jesus seems *only* to forgive the man his sins and does not cure his paralysis. At the same time, we read that the scribes in Jesus' audience are horrified at his presumption. They deem it blasphemy on Jesus' part that he claims to exercise the *divine* prerogative to forgive sins. For us, the physical cure is the most miraculous outcome, but for the scribes, the spiritual healing proposed is utterly fantastic and, in fact, not to be believed. The vital connection between these two works of power—forgiving and healing—illuminates the story and provides its lasting significance.

In Jesus' day, every spiritual and bodily infirmity was viewed as a consequence of sin. Sickness, paralysis, blindness, leprosy, demonic possession—all proceeded from the same root cause, personal or inherited sinfulness. Therefore, in the people's minds, every time Jesus healed, forgave sins, or expelled unclean spirits it was a sign that God was at work rolling back the dominion of sin and death and establishing in its place the reign of divine life and mercy. All of Christ's healing, reconciling acts—both in his early ministry and in his mission's climax on the cross—were signs of God's promised victory over sin and death. Each healing gave substance to Christ's claim that the time of fulfillment and the decisive reign of God were at hand. Jesus, as healer and forgiver of sins, showed himself to be the agent of God's Kingdom.

Jesus' action in this gospel incident is decisive. He goes right to the heart of the problem—the release of the spiritual bondage of which the physical paralysis is only a sign. In each of the five conflicts in this section of Mark's gospel, Jesus holds out the promise of fuller life. He resists those things that stunt or maim human life—paralyzed bodies, sinful lives, narrow judgments, lifeless religious practices, unconverted hearts, and closed minds. Jesus stands for compassion, reconciliation, healing, and divine intimacy. These are God's priorities; any human standards to the contrary must undergo conversion.

Sadly, by the end of the fifth conflict, it seems that the paralysis Jesus sought to dispel in the first incident has reappeared to claim new victims. This time the spiritual immobility is clearly in evidence, not hidden under the guise of physical infirmity. And this time, the paralyzed—the Pharisees—stiffen at the far-reaching mercy of Jesus and thoroughly resist his healing touch. Their behavior emerges as a cynical parody of the trusting foursome who brought their friend to Jesus. The Pharisees "kept an eye on Jesus to see whether he would heal on the sabbath, hoping to be able to bring an accusation against him" (3:2).

Jesus challenges these so-called religious leaders to exercise their teaching office wisely by distilling the essence of the sabbath law observance. "He said to them: 'Is it permitted to do a good deed on the sabbath—or an evil one? To preserve life—or to destroy it?'" (3:4). Jesus argues that the purpose of the sabbath is to promote life and the good of people; how, then, can a rigid interpretation of the law that denies life and health be consistent with the divine intention. Their stony silence angers Christ; he is "deeply grieved that they [have] closed their minds against him" (3:5). There will be no healing for them, not because Jesus does not offer it, but because their sullen self-righteousness puts a barrier between them and God's compassion. People such as these are the only hopeless cases. Refusing to admit their woundedness, they proudly rebuff the Healer's approach, preferring instead to masquerade as fit and strong.

The promise of life

The two healing stories show Christ in opposition to the narrow limits certain people would place on the compassion of God, while the three intervening stories graphically convey the full life and divine intimacy Jesus offers to those who follow him. Whatever subverts human life must submit to the judgment of Christ. Jesus is the powerful "Son of Man [who] has authority on earth to forgive sins" (2:10). He alone can accomplish the cosmic healing that is the reconciliation of the human and the divine.

The three central confrontations involve incidents where Jesus is eating with his disciples. This meal context is highly significant, for meals symbolize intimacy and communion. People do not ordinarily break the bread of their lives with just anyone! Meals are celebrations of bondedness and kinship. At a meal the very substance of life is shared, and those who partake become sharers of a common life. Both Jesus and his questioners are keenly aware of this implication.

When Jesus dines with Levi, the tax-collector-turned-disciple, and his outcast friends, some scribes of the Pharisee party are scandalized by

Christ's implicit communion with sinners. They complain: "Why does he eat with such as these?" (2:16). For them, disdaining the company of sinners is a sign of righteousness. The problem is that all—except Jesus—are sinners! If he followed the scribes' human standard of judgment, Jesus, the "Holy One of God" (1:24), should disdain *their* company as well. But that is not God's way, the way of limitless compassion and unconditional love. Jesus offers everyone a chance to repent, even these proud officials. "People who are healthy do not need a doctor; sick people do. I have *come to call sinners*, not the self-righteous" (2:17). Jesus' is a ministry of universal healing.

The *full* realization of the healing, reconciling love of God in Christ will be celebrated in the great messianic banquet of salvation to which Jesus invites all sinners. He is to be the groom, the guest of honor, the cause of rejoicing at that wedding feast! He will consummate the marriage of the human and the divine that God has been preparing throughout salvation history. Jesus reveals the union that God desires and becomes himself the bond of that intimacy. This is the good news that Jesus announces in the third controversy, the apex of Mark's conflict exposition.

Replying to the criticism that his disciples neglect fasting, Jesus declares that since a wedding is in progress, fasting is inappropriate. With the groom's eagerly awaited appearance, the wedding feast of salvation has begun! His coming suspends ordinary activity; new ways of being and behaving are the order of the day. Jesus captures the necessary response of conversion in two concrete images: new wine in old wineskins and the new patch on an old garment. The mentality that suggests making do with the old—with minor adjustments for the new—is unrealistic and tempts fate. The new wine of the Kingdom will burst the old wineskins of religious formalism with its expansive vitality and power. A thoroughgoing conversion is required; we must become new vessels in order to contain Christ's spirit. Jesus warns of the danger of trying to apply our Christianity as a new patch on our otherwise unredeemed lives. Such efforts will be both futile and destructive. Instead, we must be made new. We must "reform [our] lives and believe in the gospel" (1:15).

By sharing the bread of his presence at a meal with outcast sinners, Jesus celebrates the communion which he—as groom—has come to offer. God and sinners are united in Christ if these sinners recognize the groom's coming and respond by renewing their lives. Some trusted forms of the past, however, have become split and worn and now impede the overflowing compassion of God. These require renewal or replacement. In the final two conflicts the sabbath becomes just such a challenge.

When chided by the Pharisees for allowing his hungry disciples to pick and eat grain on the sabbath, Jesus draws a parallel between his act of authoritative compassion and that of King David. Using the Pharisees' own brand of scriptural argumentation, Jesus invites his opponents to a faith-filled perception of both the situation at hand and the underlying purpose of the sabbath. Jesus, like the revered King David, knows the ways of God and acts with divine authority. Besides aligning himself with King David—a messianic expectation in itself—Jesus stuns his Pharisaic audience by claiming: "The Son of Man is lord even of the sabbath" (2:28), that is, he is God! The sabbath is the Lord's day, and Jesus asserts his jurisdiction over it by reclaiming its divine intent: "The sabbath was made for man, not man for the sabbath" (2:27). Jesus, the Son of Man, of the line of David, is the messianic mediator of divine standards and authentic means of access to the divine. Jesus is the Way.

When Jesus defies the hard-hearted judgment of the Pharisees by curing the man's withered hand, he seals his fate and journeys toward the cross. We read: "When the Pharisees went outside, they immediately began to plot with the Herodians how they might destroy him" (3:6). The lines of conflict are drawn. Jesus makes his stand for the preservation of life (3:4) and the restoration of people to wholeness.

Jesus, Satan, and the cross

Jesus' mission and fate are further revealed as we look at the encounter of Jesus and the scribes later in chapter 3. The scribes claim that "He is possessed by Beelzebul," and "He casts out demons by the prince of demons" (3:22–23). This characterization of Jesus is the ultimate blasphemy! Jesus responds by speaking to them in parables, saying, "How can Satan drive out Satan?" And that if a kingdom or house is divided against itself it cannot survive (3:24–26). He then declares that no one can break into a strong man's house and plunder his goods unless he first binds the strong man. Only then can the house be plundered (3:27).

What is Jesus exposing here in this parable? Jesus is stating his intention to abolish the reign of the "strong man," that is, the scribal establishment represented by the demon in 1:24 (Ched Myers, *Binding the Strong Man*, pp. 166–67). "Satan cannot drive out Satan," Jesus proclaims! Jesus, in fact, is the One who has come to end the rule of Satan and to "liberate the prey of the strong and rescue the captives of the tyrants" (Is 49:24f.). He is the One who has come to establish the reign of God! This is the essence of his mission! Thus, Jesus' proclamation of God's reign, in nonviolent resistance to the rule of Satan, the established order and empire, will ultimately lead to the cross and his execution. Jesus was executed because his radical proclamation of the reign of God could not be tolerated by those in power.

Crucifixion was the primary method of capital punishment used by the Roman Empire to execute criminals, dissidents, and revolutionaries. It was the most shameful, humiliating, and excruciating form of death imaginable. Still, it did not prevent Jesus from being faithful to God and engaging in his prophetic nonviolent witness. Although Jesus experienced a torturous and agonizing death, he ultimately conquered the cross.

The cross of Christ becomes an occasion for reconciliation of the human and the divine. On the cross, Jesus hangs silently stretched between heaven and earth, a wordless parable of the reign of God overtaking a human heart, utterly transforming its frail capacities for love and sacrifice.

Jesus' death on the cross is both a radical healing and an eloquent teaching. The cross of Jesus heals the malaise of the human heart: the sick hunger for power and invincibility, the self-righteous exclusivity, the paralysis of trust, and the despair of God's promises of deliverance and new life. In place of these, Jesus teaches servanthood, humility, and forgiveness; he exemplifies the risks that open the human to the divine—faith, hope, and love. These totally accessible means of salvation light the way to God for all sinners. We do not need "to be like God"—the original temptation! We need only become like Jesus: loving, forgiving, faithful to our humanity, nonviolently resisting the forces of death and binding Satan, and consummately trusting in God.

Like Jesus on the cross, our human poverty and powerlessness, embraced and risked in loving fidelity to the plan of God, becomes salvific. God's power blazes forth in human weakness. With this realization, we can declare our own confession of who Jesus is: the Word made flesh, the Messiah, the Son of God!

DISCUSSION QUESTIONS

1. *Is there a criterion to be found in Mark's gospel that distinguishes a false conception about Jesus' identity from a true one? How do the disciples perceive him? Who do you say that Jesus is? How has your life experience affected your perception of Jesus?*

2a. *The Pharisees are not evil people, but they are led into an evil conspiracy against Jesus because they experience him as a threat. Discuss the occasions in the gospel reading when Jesus' behavior most challenges and outrages them.*

2b. *Robert Aldridge, in his article "The Courage to Start" (appendix 1, page 52), describes his experience in dealing with a similar challenge posed by his daughter. What are the values that shaped his life at work before his change? What values caused him to change his attitude and job? Identify the places in your life where your security and lifestyle are threatened by something new and challenging?*

3. *What do the healing acts of Jesus signify? What is the relationship between Jesus' acts of healing and his forgiving sins? Can you recall an experience in which your forgiving someone else—or even yourself—produced a healing power? How can the gospel dynamic of forgiveness and healing be applied to situations of international conflict?*

4. *Discuss the article's interpretation of the parables concerning new wine in old wineskins and a new patch on an old garment. What dangers does Jesus warn us about? Give specific examples. How do our habits and accustomed ways of thinking prevent us from being made new? Has your attitude toward war been made new because of your Christian belief?*

5. What are the forces of death and systems of domination that need to be "bound" and resisted today? What are some of the manifestations of the reign of God that are visible in our world today?

CLOSING REFLECTION

Mark 2:21–22

No one sews a patch of unshrunken cloth on an old cloak. If one should do so, the very thing used to cover the hole would pull away—the new from the old—and the tear would get worse. Similarly, no person pours new wine into old wineskins. If one does so the wine will burst the skins and both wine and skins will be lost. No, new wine is poured into new skins.

The journey of discipleship

OPENING PRAYER

Dearest Jesus, you ask us to journey with you to the heart of fidelity—the cross. Accept our desire to follow you, and help us overcome our residual fears of following in your path of ultimate service and sacrifice. Like Peter, we long to boldly confess you before our brothers and sisters in this world, but too often we share his blindness and resistance to the cross. Empower us to take risks of faith for your sake and for the gospel, to risk laying down our lives and our instruments of destruction in the belief that you will not leave us in death but will raise us to new life. In disarming our hearts of fear, arrogance, and the need to "lord it over" others, may we come to that trusting openness that sees you in every child of God and rejoices to welcome you there. In welcoming you in our midst now, may we grow more like you and learn from you what it means to "take up the cross and follow in [your] steps." This we pray in struggle, remembering your mercy. Amen.

GOSPEL READING

Mark 8:22–38; 9:30–37; 10:32–52 (for a shorter reading: 8:27–38)

DISCUSSION ARTICLE ✠ *The journey of discipleship*

Our journey of discipleship begins when we, like Peter at Caesarea Philippi (8:29), confess our belief that Jesus is the Messiah and Lord of life. Upon making this initial confession, the lifelong journey of faith and conversion is inaugurated. For once we perceive who Jesus is, we must then take up his cross and follow in his steps. As disciples, we journey from the fringes of faith, where liberation is bountifully promised, to the heart of faithfulness, where liberation is wondrously fulfilled in servanthood, the giving of life for others. Jesus assures us that in responding to his call the path of discipleship will lead to new life.

Mark's journey narrative in chapters 8–10 through ten contains the heart of Christ's instruction on discipleship. On his way from Galilee, the place of the marginalized, to Jerusalem, the center of Jewish life and worship, Jesus painstakingly teaches the meaning of his life and death. Here in the city that kills the prophets, he equips his followers for the arduous but rewarding path of gospel fidelity. Three times Jesus predicts his suffering, death, and resurrection, and three times his disciples resist the idea that Jesus the Messiah must also be the Suffering Servant. Each time, in turn, Jesus patiently teaches his baffled disciples the divine values of forgiveness, trust, and unconditional love. As prophet and messiah, Jesus is charged with the vitality of his mission: to proclaim God's reign and to heal the ravages of sin and death. It is in his fundamental commitment to usher in the Kingdom of Life that he knowingly accepts the risk of the cross.

His cross teaches us that death is vanquished not by a convincing display of divine might but by the power of a humble, forgiving heart surrendered totally to God in love for others. Whenever we open ourselves to the power of the cross, the Kingdom stirs within us. Its power disrupts our lives, challenges our most basic assumptions, and brings us in touch with the root of our being. Our view of the world and of ourselves is transformed. Then the life of the Kingdom compels us to break down the barriers that separate us, to become vulnerable to the needs of others, and to serve them by walking in the path of the cross.

For Mark, the journey of discipleship requires a conversion from blindness to sight. The evangelist's account of Jesus' journey to Jerusalem not only contains the basic instruction for true discipleship but also reveals the blindness and resistance of the disciples to the mission and cross of Jesus. Mark emphasizes the disciples' spiritual blindness by enclosing the narrative of the three passion predictions with two stories of blind men being healed: the blind man at Bethsaida (8:22–26) and Bartimaeus (10:46–52). It is their utter faith in this stranger, Jesus, that enables his healing power to be present in them and to affect them. Their blindness and cure stand in relief to the symbolic blindness of the disciples, who again and again reject the efficacy of the cross.

In our age, we too struggle with the problem of often failing to grasp the significance of Jesus' mission. The very existence of nuclear weapons in our society is a profound manifestation of our own moral and spiritual blindness. Our intention to use these weapons fully contradicts Jesus' teachings and his suffering and death on the cross. To confront this nuclear intention as people of faith is to expose, confess, and overcome this evil.

Like the blind Bethsaidan whose cure takes repeated applications of Christ's healing hands, and like the Twelve, who require three passion predictions to open their eyes to the power and wisdom of the cross, we contemporary disciples need to be continuously touched and taught by Christ. Our efforts to overcome our moral and spiritual blindness and to be sustained by faith in this nuclear age rest on our choice to be touched by Jesus and to follow his way of the cross.

Lessons in discipleship

At the turning point of the gospel when, for the first time, one of the disciples is able to say of Jesus publicly, "You are the Messiah" (8:29), Jesus seizes the opportunity to instruct his disciples on the *real* meaning of his messiahship. "He began to teach them that the Son of Man had to suffer much, be rejected by the elders, the chief priests, and the scribes, be put to death, and rise three days later" (8:31). This prospect appalls Peter. He resists it, takes Jesus aside, and tries to dissuade him from the way of the cross. Jesus' reaction to Peter's appeal is stunning. "Get out of my sight, you satan! You are not judging by God's standards but by man's" (8:33). The vehemence of Christ's words sobers us and makes us note all the more carefully the source of Jesus' anger: Peter, although he recognizes Jesus as the Messiah, finds it unthinkable that the Christ should have to suffer. By his response, Peter shows himself blind to the healing and saving power that the free gift of one's life for others can achieve. Peter, like all disciples, must be taught *Jesus'* way of salvation, the way of the Kingdom. The disciple is still thinking in the categories of the world; he prefers the path of security and untroubled glory to Christ's way of love and humble servanthood.

A second and third time, Jesus tries to break through the disciples' inability to see and teach the way that the Kingdom will come—life-giving sacrifice. Each time, Jesus' predictions of his saving death/resurrection receives scant response. The pathos of a man filled with the vitality of life and love who nonetheless embraces death for the sake of his loved ones is the stuff of great tragedy, yet the disciples seem unmoved and uncomprehending. The paradox of Jesus' messiahship—that God's Son should have to give his life in ransom for theirs—is too much for them, so they lapse into more manageable concerns. On both occasions they begin to argue among themselves about who is the greatest. Their ambition for prestige and places of glory is the exact counterpoint of Jesus' self-revelation as Suffering Servant. He promises to give of himself to the point of death, while his followers vie for positions of security and influence.

The teachings Jesus offers each time he promises his own life for the sake of others are difficult for the worldly power-seeking disciples to grasp. Even as they follow him in his journey, they close their eyes to the risk of sacrifice, to the risk of the cross. Jesus patiently teaches that unless we deny ourselves by emptying our hearts of self-centered ambition, begin to spend ourselves as he did in the service of our brothers and sisters, and nonviolently resist systemic evil, domination, and death, we cannot call ourselves his followers. However, if we *do* risk losing our lives in servanthood, we are promised that the self-denial will yield ultimate self-fulfillment. We will preserve our lives in the sight of God and assure ourselves of places with Christ in his kingdom. The alternative is grim. If we reject the cross and seek to preserve our lives by any means other than union with Jesus' path of servanthood, we risk alienation from Christ (8:31) and exile from his Kingdom.

In contrast to the disciples' desire to be greatest, Jesus identifies himself with a child and declares that the quality of our welcome for the smallest and the least is the measure of our welcome for him. Christ depicts himself as the child of the loving God unwelcomed in our midst so long as the weak, the poor, the disenfranchised, and the powerless of this world are despised and neglected. We learn that in welcoming these marginal multitudes, these global Galileans, we gain access not only to Christ but also to the One who sent him. The living God is touched by our welcoming the poor. Suddenly, servanthood assumes new proportions: no longer is it simply justice or charity; it is consummate worship. Welcoming the least becomes serving the greatest!

Still Jesus' disciples are unable to see the transforming power God reveals when humble service is coupled with trusting love. The ways of might and domination prevalent among the powerful of their day tempt them to mistrust lowliness. Jesus counters: "It cannot be like that with you. Anyone who aspires to greatness must serve the needs of all. The Son of Man has come not to be served but to serve—to give his life in ransom for the many" (10:43–45). Humility, servanthood, and love are the only forces strong enough to break the grip of sin and death. To be the greatest, to be the saving Lord of history, Jesus will take the place of a condemned man—and there serve the needs of all sinners. Christ's followers too must be prepared to welcome such a status and share such a life.

Moral blindness and the nuclear intention
The cross of the Suffering Servant heals our vision and opens our minds and hearts. Like the disciples, however, we often resist Jesus' teaching on servanthood as well as the cross it implies: we prefer to dominate rather than to serve others. No event in our age more significantly demonstrates our blindness toward Christ's values of unconditional forgiveness and love than the creation of nuclear weapons by the state. We have become morally blind to this evil which continues to be justified in the name of "national security." This dependence on nuclear weapons for our ultimate "security" as a nation is known as nuclearism.

By their very nature nuclear weapons are genocidal instruments of mass murder and indiscriminate destruction. A single nuclear weapon has the capacity to destroy an entire city of people in a few seconds by blast and fire. It's cancer-causing and genetic consequences would affect all biological life in a wider area virtually forever. Many of the over 13,400 nuclear weapons on earth today *individually* contain a greater destructive power than the combined effect of all of the weapons so far used in human history. The mining, testing, production, and deployment of these weapons have desecrated native lands and the Marshall and South Pacific Islands and have caused incalculable ecological devastation to God's creation.

Despite this level of violence, two of the most powerful governments on earth continue to possess massive nuclear arsenals. Although the US and Russia have reduced their arsenals, they still have between them about 12,600 nuclear weapons. And both countries are modernizing and expanding their nuclear forces. Their mutually reinforcing nuclear war policies are still extremely dangerous. Each side possesses a first-strike capability, with many weapons on "hair-trigger alert." At any moment, these weapons, by direct order or miscalculation, could be used. As the two nations reshape their arsenals and strategies, and with the ongoing problem of nuclear proliferation, nuclear war, as unthinkable as it is, becomes increasingly probable. Furthermore, these nuclear war preparations are all legally sanctioned by the superpowers and nuclear nations, despite international treaties that prohibit the use, threatened use, and, now, possession of nuclear weapons.

The destructive potential of nuclear war is so vast that we cannot comprehend the extent of the evil we have created and have allowed to rule over us. Our attempts to define, to understand, even to control in some ways this capacity to destroy do not bring us any closer to the conscientious moment of confessing and resisting the basic evil.

Nuclear weapons derive from a long history of human sinfulness—from the first time brother killed brother. The sin of moral blindness wraps itself around the basic death intention obscuring at its heart the ultimate sin nurtured there: the choice of death over life. To be credible, the threat of using nuclear weapons presupposes the intention of using them. This nuclear intention is morally indefensible because what is wrong to do is wrong to threaten to do. It recommends global suicide as a solution to the problems of competing ideologies and economic interests. This murderous intention openly betrays the intention of the cross: the willingness of Christ to suffer and die for others so that they might live the fullness of his Kingdom.

The nuclear intention is the central violence of our age to which all violence is linked. The violence of starvation and poverty; the violence against the earth; the violence against children, women, and the unborn; the violence of racism; the violence of state torture, imprisonment, and execution; the violence of the street; and the subtle violence of our affluent lifestyle are all drawn together and reenacted in the cold, dark nuclear intention.

Healed vision and the vision of healing

The stories of blind eyes being opened reveal both the power of faith that healing requires and the power of love that healing becomes. This healing marks the loss of spiritual isolation and remoteness and the recovery of moral insight: the ability to see things as they are, to gain an orientation guided by the values of the Kingdom rather than by those of the world.

To discern with open, willful eyes the nuclear intention that we hold within us is to confess our own complicity in the central violence of our age. To behold this evil perpetuated through human history and contaminating the human spirit is to ask God to forgive us for something we fear is too terrible to forgive, too large and complex for us to undo even with God's help. But when we are touched by the healing power of the cross, we see ourselves revealed as both nuclear victims and sinners, although we do not want to be either. Our blindness to the reality of nuclear weapons and to our responsibility for them enables us to hide this terrible sin, thus compounding it. Like Peter, we ask Christ to be reasonable, to be reconciled with worldly values even though they have produced in our time the means to destroy every living thing on earth.

True sight comes gradually for us, as it did for the nameless Bethsaidan. Jesus patiently asks us, again and again: "Can you see anything?" Somehow our blindness has heightened our sense of touch: we recognize in the strong though gentle hands of Christ a healing power that we know can transform our vision and our lives. There is an unexpected intimacy to the feel of these crucified hands. His touch penetrates the scars left from past wounds, exposes and opens our hearts, and enables us to risk vulnerable love. By inviting the hands of Christ to cover our face, we confess the spiritual blindness that afflicts us personally and as a society, and we dare to ask for the eyes of faith that will see through the false values we had embraced. The risk of confession, of repentance, becomes the invitation to wholeness, to healing.

To overcome our inability to see, we must be prepared to journey to be healed and then to journey further once healed. The journey is both the test and consequence of faith. It can lead us through unfamiliar terrain, even to Jerusalem and the cross. Yet Christ's healing touch impels a journey filled with a longing for the Kingdom. We move away from the sick place of our hearts in following the One whose act of heart—the cross—transforms us. Our eyes of faith perceive this cross of Jesus as the instrument of healing and new life for all.

DISCUSSION QUESTIONS

1a. Is the cross a frightening symbol for you? How does it change in meaning when it is linked with the resurrection (as Jesus links them in his three passion predictions)? How is it possible to think of the cross as a symbol of life and healing? What are the most visible signs of the cross and resurrection that you see today?

1b. What does Christ's death and resurrection teach us about the nature of power—the power of the world and the power of the Kingdom? Which power was more real to the disciples? Which is more real to you? Is the cross a symbol of power or powerlessness—or both? Is the world's notion of peace through military strength compatible with the way of the cross?

2. To be a servant is a lowly status according to the standards of the world. Why is there special dignity in the servanthood to which the gospel calls us? What power is being served? What practical results does this service hope to achieve? Why must the servant be prepared to suffer? What concrete examples do you know of in which someone's willing self-sacrifice has promoted the life of another?

3a. Throughout history threats of violence have continually been carried out—war is a constant human experience. Do you believe that the threat to use nuclear weapons is rooted in the full intention to use them? What is your response to the information listed in appendix 2 (pages 59–65, 77–79), especially the Nuclear Weapons Timeline and the occasions when the US threatened to use nuclear weapons? Is this intention merely a feature of international policy, or does it stem more deeply from the human heart? Can you identify this intention as being yours personally? If so, how can you struggle to remove it? What does this intention have to do with power? What does it have to do with the cross?

3b. Do you believe, as the article suggests, that the nuclear intention is morally connected to every act of violence in our culture? Discuss the ways in which the violence of nuclear weapons is related to the violence we see in our society.

4. What is your response to Pope Francis' condemnation of the "possession" of nuclear weapons (see appendix 3, page 90)? If it is wrong to possess nuclear weapons, then it is wrong to be involved in their production, maintenance, and use. What are the concrete actions that we, our parish, and our church can take to withdraw our consent from the possession and use of nuclear weapons?

5. What do we learn from the contrast between the blind men who were healed and the twelve who persistently resisted Christ's teaching about this messiahship? What prevented the disciples from comprehending the way of the cross and Jesus' role as Suffering Servant? In what ways are we like the struggling disciples? In what ways does our nuclear intention reveal us as morally and spiritually impaired? Why is it so difficult to want to see? What risks must we be willing to take so that we may be healed of our lack of vision? What can we learn from the action of Bartimaeus and the Bethsaidan?

CLOSING REFLECTION

Mark 8:34–36

Jesus summoned the crowd with his disciples and said to them: If you wish to come after me, you must deny your very self, take up your cross, and follow in my steps. Whoever would preserve one's life will lose it, but whoever loses one's life for my sake and the gospel's will preserve it. What profit does a person show who gains the whole world but is destroyed in the process?

To trust in God's promise

OPENING PRAYER

*Loving God, we have broken so many promises we made to you. Yet you keep
your promises to us. Enable us to recognize more clearly and fully the power of
the promise you make, the promise of Jesus to heal us, the promise of the Spirit
who stirs in our hearts. We pray that we may see your word as a promise for
each day, each moment, each experience. Help us, dear God, to renounce the
false promises we make to ourselves, the false gods we create in our midst when
we dare to doubt your promise. Increase in us a trust in the promise of life that
you bring, not in the promise of death that we in our failure depend on. Help
us to become more trustful and forgiving of others—and of ourselves—more
prayerful in all that we do. We ask this in the name of Jesus, your Son, who
trusts us more than we know. Amen.*

GOSPEL READING

Mark 11:11–25

DISCUSSION ARTICLE ✢ *To trust in God's promise*

Jesus' nonviolent demonstration in the temple marks the high point of
Jesus' confrontation with the religious authorities of his day. This bold
action of cleansing the temple contrasts dramatically with the course of
events it precipitates, the *passion* of the cross. This contrast of a disrup-

tive Jesus in the temple and a suffering Jesus on the cross accentuates the judgment that he offers in both moments. His is a judgment and a call to the people in the tradition of the prophets of Israel to return to the way of God.

Jesus' indignation toward the empty formalism of the temple is prefigured in the story in which he curses the fig tree. In juxtaposing these stories Mark interprets both the displeasure of Jesus and the hypocrisy of the temple that it reveals. The tree symbolically illustrates the organic quality of the temple as institution. It is the house of worship with a living tradition, whose roots are watered in the promise of the messiah, a promise ever renewed. The tree is special in Jesus' view—he notices it in the distance and goes out of the way to examine it. He searches the tree for a sign of early fruit, a sign and promise of the fullness of summer to come. But the tree yields no early fruit, just foliage. Jesus does not curse the tree for its frailty or lack of form—this tree is mature and covered with leaves—but rather for its lack of fruit, its lack of achievement.

The cleansing of the temple
The temple stands fruitless before Jesus, who inspects everything in its precincts upon entering Jerusalem (11:11). No fruitful worship, no sign of an authentic messianic expectation is evident. The prayer and ritual sacrifice of the temple are revealed to be merely gesture and form devoid of an inner faith. In prophetic witness Jesus overturns the tables of the merchants and money-changers whose business profanes the temple. The same hands that opened blind eyes send the wood crashing to the stone.

Jesus' disruption of temple commerce is meant to clean away all that defiles the temple and subverts true worship. In its abuses temple worship deadens the spirit of the covenant it claims through tradition. Its cleansing represents Jesus' attempt to reclaim the house of God to true prayer by exposing the hypocrisy and spiritual blindness of external religious practices that have no spiritual content.

Jesus' witness reflects, as well, his response to the injustices caused by the arrangement of temple power: the social privilege, the system of domination that puts the religious authorities above others as a temple class. Jesus' demonstration occurs in the outer court of the Gentiles, the large margin of space that surrounds the priestly sanctuary of prayer and ritual sacrifice. The cleansing thus becomes a demand both for true worship and for justice—justice for the marginal, for the unchosen Gentiles, for the outcasts of Galilee, whose holy space is given over to the worldly interest of the privileged. Jesus cites the prophet Isaiah: "My house shall be called a house of prayer for all peoples" (11:17). The cleansing of the temple follows the call of divine obedience and becomes, at the same time, a radical call for human justice.

"On what authority are you doing these things? Who has given you the power to do them?" (11:28). This is the question with which the religious authorities accuse Christ. For Christ, the temple cleansing directs the very question of authority to the defenders of empty orthodoxy. On what authority is religious expression emptied of faith? On what authority are the injustices of poverty and inequality tolerated? In proclaiming God's singular authority, Jesus challenges us to remove everything that stands in the way of the Kingdom.

Nuclear trust

On what authority—divine or human—do we rely on nuclear weapons for our freedom and security? How can we reconcile our nuclear trust, our faith in the threat of total death, with our trust in a merciful God?

Any trust that we put in nuclear weapons is trust displaced from God. Our dependence on the nuclear threat to maintain our own personal national security represents in itself our most profound doubt in the power of God to heal and free us. We trust more in the power of fear and death than we do in the power of forgiveness and life; destruction is the means we seek and the outcome we have come to expect. The nuclear plot is a statement of utter despair, of divine mistrust, of radical doubt in the promise of God and in the healing power of the cross.

Our trust in nuclear weapons conceals a false, messianic promise—liberation and security by death-dealing. The bomb becomes a substitute god, an idol to which godlike authority is assigned. We surround it with an atmosphere of mystery, reverence, and finality. We trust in these weapons to save us. We forget God's intention for the world and violate it by nurturing the death intention in our hearts.

Our nuclear trust is an abomination to the holy, an expression of our faithlessness as a people. "Nuclearism" has virtually become a national religion. It constitutes idolatry. If our nuclear trust is meant to safeguard our freedom to express our faith in Christ, then there *is no* true faith—there is only the temple profaned.

The activity of the world reflects the activity in our hearts. Our weak human hearts invite this violence to take root within them, but there is no yield of fruit, only the withering of our spirits. Insofar as we, a religious people, have supported in our hearts and in the structures of society this threat of absolute destruction, we ourselves have built and sustained an unclean temple. This nuclear temple of our day begs for a courageous, cleansing Christ.

In whom do we trust?

The struggle of the disciples to overcome their blindness to the meaning of Christ's messianic suffering resembles the problem of discipleship in the nuclear age. Our task is first to discern the messianic qualities with which we have endowed the technology of self-destruction and then to renounce this false worship by turning to and trusting God.

Jesus comforts us with the simple words: "Fear is useless. What is needed is trust" (5:36). This admonition speaks to our blindness of heart and invites us to confess and renounce the nuclear intention that we hide there. Jesus, who brings the gift of life, assures us that God can be trusted and that "all things are possible" in a trusting relationship with God (10:27).

The morning after the temple cleaning, Jesus and his disciples pass the fig tree he had cursed, now withered to its roots. Responding to their amazement he instructs them on the merits of trustfulness and prayer. "Put your trust in God....I give you my word, if you are ready to believe that you will receive whatever you ask for in prayer, it shall be done for you. When you stand to pray, forgive anyone against whom you have a grievance so that your heavenly Father may in turn forgive you your faults" (11:22, 24–25).

Jesus calls us to the simple but complete trustfulness of a child. He reminds us that faithfulness consists in expecting and accepting gifts from God and in seeing others as gifts and becoming gift to them. Our nuclear trust relationship violates this gift quality of a life of faith. Our death trust kills the vital expectation of gift from the "God of the living" (12:27).

Expectation is the fruit of trustfulness and prayer; it ripens in the form of vigilance. "Learn a lesson from the fig tree," Jesus teaches. "Once the sap of its branches runs high and it begins to sprout leaves, you know that summer is near" (13:28). In fruitful faith we must await God's promise to return and come to see the interim promise of gifts fulfilled. In nurturing the seeds of our faith, we ourselves become the gift of God. Jesus, the Expected One, urges us to be "constantly on the watch," to have eyes of faith, to avoid dead vision (13:33–34). Watchfulness is the response to Christ's gift of open eyes.

Implicit in the trustful expectancy of prayer is the willingness to forgive others their wrongs and, perhaps more deeply, to forgive ourselves for the wrong of a misplaced trust. Honest prayer and true justice, Christ's motives for cleansing the temple of our hearts, are based on these aspects of inner and outer forgiveness.

The trust and forgiveness to which Jesus calls us radically subverts our dependency on nuclear weapons. Our trust in God cannot admit a vengeful trust in death-dealing; our forgiveness of brothers and sisters precludes the choice of nuclear murder.

In the new relationship that he offers and becomes, Jesus promises us that prayer can realize a genuine freedom and peace. He insists that forgiveness conditions prayer, that the forgiveness of others secures our own forgiveness before God. Our relationship to God is inseparable from our relationship to one another. This mutuality of relationships—to God and to neighbor—reflects the integration of divine and human aspects in Jesus' own identity and in his passion and action of the cross. In the shadow of the cross, he teaches the great but simple commandment of love—the mutual aspects of love that true faithfulness enables.

A scribe approaches Jesus with the question: "Which is the first of all commandments?" Jesus replies: "This is the first: 'Hear, O Israel! The Lord our God is Lord alone! Therefore you shall love the Lord your God with all your heart, with all your soul, with all your mind, and with all your strength.' This is the second: 'You shall love your neighbor as yourself.' There is no other commandment greater than these" (12:29–31). "Excellent Teacher!"

the scribe remarks, such love of God and neighbor is "worth more than any burnt offering or sacrifice" (12:33). The scribe perceives the wisdom of Jesus' words. No sacrifice, no temple cult, can replace the virtue of true worship and justice, the love of God and of each person. This commandment unites the divine trust and the human forgiveness that Christ imparts and invites.

DISCUSSION QUESTIONS

1. Does Jesus' action in cleansing the temple seem uncharacteristic to you? How are his actions there consistent with his role as Suffering Servant? Do you think people watching Jesus were positively or negatively affected? Who were those positively affected? Who was negatively affected? Are there Christians today acting in a similarly disruptive fashion in pursuing the goals of the gospel?

2a. Everyone is tempted to idol worship, even Christians. What is idolatry? What are the idols that are most often worshiped in our society? In what way are nuclear weapons an expression of our idol worship? Who are the sacrificial victims? Who are the beneficiaries?

2b. Whom do we trust? Where do we ultimately find our security? What kind of trust does our nuclear weapons policies reflect (see 2018 US Nuclear Posture Review in appendix 2, pages 66–68)? Is this trust consistent with the gospel message? Discuss how the statements in appendix 3 (pages 81–99) attempt to answer these questions?

3. Discuss some threatening situations you experience in everyday life. What feelings do you experience when threatened? How do you imagine the feelings your aggressor has toward you? What are some Christian ways of dealing with these feelings? Do you think such interpersonal solutions have parallels on an international level? In light of these considerations, do you think that the Christian pacifist stance in a world of nuclear weapons is naive and impractical? What is ultimately at stake for the pacifist? What is at stake in the variety of other nonpacifist attitudes? What is your response to the Catholic Nonviolent Initiative Appeal in appendix 5 (pages 114–18)?

4. When we pray about particular things, prayer more often changes us and our relationship to these things than it does the things themselves. When we pray for world peace, therefore, we pray largely about changing ourselves. What are the concrete changes we hope for when we pray for peace?

CLOSING REFLECTION

Mark 11:24–25
I give you my word, if you are ready to believe that you will receive whatever you ask for in prayer, it shall be done for you. When you stand to pray, forgive anyone against whom you have a grievance so that your heavenly Father may in turn forgive you your faults.

To risk eucharistic love

OPENING PRAYER

Lord Jesus, without seeing you, we believe that you have come to us in the sign of your body broken, your blood poured out. We hold before you, Lord, this world we live in, a world for which we share responsibility with so many sisters and brothers. Today our world is plagued by weapons of destruction that threaten to annihilate all life God has created. Under the earth, in the oceans, above our heads in planes—thousands of nuclear weapons betray our lack of faithfulness in your eucharistic love and in the gospel call to be peacemakers.

What do you think, Lord, as you look at what we are doing? Jesus, we hear you say that if the human family is to survive, we will have to take a position for God's family. We will have to measure what we have, and what our country has, against those who are victims of starvation and gross neglect. We will have to lay down our fear of the "enemy" for, through you, all people are members of the one body. We will have to renounce the nuclear intention in our hearts and strive to break open the blessed bread of our lives and share it with others.

Jesus, help us to change our hearts and to risk accepting the gift of your Eucharist. Deepen our trust in your guidance, and give us the strength to witness your cross. Enable us to be visible signs of your eucharistic love in this nuclear age. As we seek to be your faithful followers, empower us to give our lives—as you did—in love and service. All glory and praise be to you, Lord Jesus, bread of everlasting life, now and forever. Amen.

Mark 14:17–31

DISCUSSION ARTICLE ☩ *To risk eucharistic love*

In the eucharistic bread and wine Jesus offers us his Body and Blood. These simple elements of the human meal convey a deep sense of intimacy: this food is offered as a personal gift, to be taken to the most interior part of our being. The Eucharist is food that endures—a gift of love that continually renews our hearts.

The Eucharist conveys a love we cannot contain, a love that overwhelms our hearts and our ability to understand it. Not to express this love in turn to one another, even in our often slow and fragile ways, is to renounce it. God places on us who receive this love the demand that we share it with others, especially those who, like us, are most in need of it. The fundamental character of love is that it be given to others in order to receive it fully. This is central to Jesus' teachings on servanthood and the healing cross. In this way, the Eucharist and the cross are related healing moments.

There is a confessional aspect to our sharing in this banquet: we confess our unworthiness to be present at the table. We know the unique brokenness hidden within us. Yet with trust in the Healer we carry our brokenness openly to the table as we take our place there in celebration. The Eucharist is a meal for sinners, not the self-righteous. Jesus comes to fill the hungry, not the fed; to heal the sick, not those who are well (2:17). It is the poor, the broken in body and spirit, who follow him, who are drawn to the Healer and Teacher. He welcomes them—us—and transforms our poverty into wholeness.

The Eucharist in the midst of betrayal and denial
When we recognize the predictions of betrayal and denial that surround this holy meal, we become aware of how immense and resilient is Jesus' love. On the evening he is betrayed by Judas, denied by Peter, and abandoned by the rest, Jesus nonetheless offers them the bread and wine of Eucharist, symbols of his life poured out in love.

Jesus begins this sacred liturgy of self-sacrifice by telling his disciples, "One of you is about to betray me, yes, one who is eating with me—accursed be that man" (14:18). Without hesitation, the disciples sorrowfully respond to Jesus, one by one, saying, "Surely not I" (14:19). As on the journey to Jerusalem, the disciples are determined to remain true to their Lord. Yet deep down, in the recesses of their hearts, they still resist the "cup of suffering" that Jesus calls them to. They still cannot accept the cross as the way to wholeness and new life. While out of failure to recognize their weakness and their impending trial, the disciples say, "Surely not I"—we will always remain loyal—the actual test of faith results in their rejection and abandonment of Jesus.

Just as the disciples strive to be faithful to Jesus and then lose faith in times of trial, we contemporary Christians are also prone to failures in fidelity. During moments when we assume we are in control, we can testify that no matter what situation arises, we will remain faithful. Yet when we are directly in the midst of crisis and tension, we give way to fear and worry about our status and security. We substitute the human values of expediency and self-interest for the divine values of patience and unconditional love.

In contrast, Jesus, with foreknowledge that he will be betrayed and denied by his disciples, still offers them his body and blood. By becoming human and identifying with the suffering and marginalized, Jesus knows the human condition. He knows that we fail in faith and need forgiveness and understanding. In expressing the patient, untiring love he has for us, the gift of the Eucharist becomes the ultimate expression of Jesus' love and forgiveness. Amid his disciples' failure of faith and resistance to the cross— then and now—Jesus extends with open hands this life-giving bread and saving cup.

"Can you drink the cup?"

Jesus offers us his all-embracing love in the Eucharist and awaits our response. Can we accept this unconditional love? Are we willing to give our love freely to others in the way Jesus exemplifies? Can we drink from the cup of suffering that Jesus must drink, so that with him we can be transformed to new life (10:39)?

At the eucharistic meal, Jesus prepares himself as well as his disciples for the road to Calvary. He reveals the imminent suffering and death he would endure by sharing with them crushed wheat and grapes. In lifting up these simple earthly elements, he anticipates his being crushed to become the blood of a new Passover covenant. The covenant he now begins will be completed in the messianic banquet of salvation. Jesus assures us of the salvation he will gain: "Never again will I drink of the fruit of the vine until I drink it new in the reign of God" (14:22–24).

In offering the Eucharist to his disciples on this holy Feast of Unleavened Bread, Jesus reenacts the Passover story. The Passover meal recalls the exodus of the people of Israel from Egypt, the land of slavery. It commemorates God's deliverance of the Hebrew people from the chains of ruthless oppression and recounts their journey of faith to the promised land. Jesus inaugurates a new Passover through the sharing of Eucharist in the shadow of the cross. For by his death on the cross all people are delivered from the bondage of sin and death and are offered access to the promised land of salvation. Thus, the Last Supper reveals to us that Jesus is the deliverer of the new Passover.

For Christians, to receive this new Passover meal is to accept the cross that is our means of liberation. Our taking the cup means that we, like Jesus, must be willing to be servants of one another and to embrace the great commandment of love. We must be willing to make the sacrifice God requires of us. We must be able to recognize with Jesus that it is through totally giving our lives to serve God and one another, and through resisting all forms of injustice and violence, that we can be made new people. This total abandonment of self led Jesus to the cross. Whenever we partake in the Eucharist, then, Jesus asks us if we can drink the cup of suffering that he drinks and journey with him to the cross.

Living the Eucharist

The sacred meal of the Eucharist gives us the strength and nourishment we need to confront and be healed of the evils within us and around us. In our day, as we seek to embody the love Jesus gives to us in the Eucharist and to be converted to the way of his cross, we are faced with great challenges. What does it mean to participate in the Eucharist with a nuclear intention in our hearts and our missiles aimed at our sisters and brothers? Can our nuclear intention be reconciled with the communion that this Eucharist celebrates?

The nuclear intention embodies fear, not love. This intention clearly rejects the love Jesus extends to us in the eucharistic meal. It directly contradicts the healing spirit that the Eucharist seeks to foster. If, as Christians, we truly accept the Eucharist and cross of Jesus, how can we possibly contemplate, much less condone, the premeditated mass murder of sisters and brothers in Christ! The threat of nuclear murder defiles the Eucharist and rejects the healing love of Christ. To build such weapons of mass murder and to intend to use them is a sin against God and the human family.

The nuclear intention rooted in our heart and the worldwide proliferation of murderous weapons it has spawned claim hosts of victims each day. These are the victims of gross neglect, the starving of the world, many of whom are children, the little ones whom Jesus would welcome and touch (10:13). These victims are the marginal, the Galilean poor whose company he sought. They, the unfed, the diseased, the poor, become the holy innocents, living sacrifices before the nuclear idol.

How can we reconcile the victimhood of the starving and the suffering with our taking a place at the table with Jesus? What does it mean to accept this eucharistic food while millions of sisters and brothers starve?

The eucharistic love that Jesus shares with us implies a risk. The mandate of eucharistic love is to be united with Christ and with one another. Despite the modern circumstances of betrayal and denial we face, we hear Jesus calling us to be servants of one another, members of his one body. When one person suffers, we all suffer. As Christ had compassion for the hungry multitudes (6:30–44 and 8:1–10), we too are called to help feed one another. In fact, we are called to be Eucharist for one another in the midst of betrayal and denial. To be blessed, broken, and given for one another is to risk love at all costs.

Jesus died as he lived. With his arms outstretched on the cross, totally disarmed, he embraces all humanity with his infinite, merciful love. Christ invites all of God's people to choose the path of love and self-sacrifice, which is the way of nonviolence, the true means of justice and peace. By identifying with the Suffering Servant, reconciliation and healing can occur between warring nations. Our allegiance to Jesus requires that we renounce our nuclear intention and remove the scandal of starvation from our world.

Faced with the violence of human starvation and nuclear annihilation, we blindly insist, "Surely not I, Lord!" At this moment Jesus offers us—as he did his disciples—communion in his mission of servanthood. United with Christ's sacrificial love, the hope of redemption and deliverance dawns anew for our world. We need only to risk incarnating the love of the Eucharist and place our complete trust in God. For Jesus assures us that "with God all things are possible" (10:27).

DISCUSSION QUESTIONS

1a. The Eucharist signifies our human brokenness and Christ's life broken for us on the cross. Discuss the particular ways in which this brokenness is manifest in the world, in our lives, in the lives of those we know, and in all the things that keep people separated and in fear. How do we all share in the disciples' betrayal of Christ?

1b. The Eucharist also signifies the spiritual food that nourishes us and brings us to wholeness and health. What vision for the world does the Eucharist present to the believer? Who belongs at the table? Who is to be fed? Who is to provide? The promises of the Kingdom are beyond our wildest imaginings, so imagine boldly: What hopes for the world and for yourselves do you bring in coming to the Eucharist? Is there a risk in receiving the Eucharist if our aims are not consonant with Christ's?

2. Receiving the Eucharist unites us in Christ's universal, forgiving love. How, then, can we reconcile the presence of Christ's love in the Eucharist with our society's nuclear intention? Are there ways in which we can extend this eucharistic love as a healing force in a world of conflict and division?

3. While $738 billion was allocated for the 2020 US military budget, thousands of people suffer and die daily from neglect and lack of basic necessities. In 2019 nuclear weapons expenditures by the nine nuclear nations were an estimated $72.9 billion—funds that could instead be used to reverse climate change, eliminate poverty, and address other social and economic needs. Who profits from these weapons? Discuss the connection between nuclear weapons and the problem of poverty, racism, world hunger, adequate health care and housing for all the world's poor, and other unmet human need(s) (see appendix 4, pages 102–106). Do you think our concern for security—both personally and as a nation—would become less and less important if we were willing to provide more and more for the just needs of the world's poor? In what ways can the Eucharist enable us to share what we have with those who have little or nothing?

4. Do you feel hopeful that nuclear war can be averted? Does your Christian faith contribute to the sense of hope that you might have? What changes do you think you can make in your life to work toward eliminating the threat of nuclear war? How can you, your faith community/congregation, and the wider Church bring about disarmament and convert the war economy? What is your response to the articles in appendix 5 (pages 107–13, 118–20)?

5. What is your response to Pope Francis' 2017 World Day of Peace Message: "Nonviolence: A Style of Politics for Peace" in appendix 3 (page 86–89)? What would happen if a nonviolent framework were truly adopted by all the nations of the world to resolve conflict?

CLOSING REFLECTION

Mark 14:22–25

During the meal he took bread, blessed and broke it, and gave it to them. "Take this," he said, "this is my body." He likewise took a cup, gave thanks and passed it to them, and they all drank from it. He said to them, "This is my blood, the blood of the covenant, to be poured out on behalf of many. I solemnly assure you, I will never again drink of the fruit of the vine until the day when I drink it new in the reign of God."

A liturgy of life

CALL TO WORSHIP

Let us seek to renew our commitment to follow Jesus, our crucified and risen Lord, by lifting up our lives in prayerful worship before God.

OPENING PRAYER

Nearing the end of our journey together, we echo the prayer of the blind Bartimaeus: "Jesus, son of David, have mercy on [us]!" Our hearts are both burdened and blessed. The weight of our starving brothers and sisters, the enormity of our nuclear intention, and the ponderous danger of our nuclear arsenals bring us to our knees in prayer. Yet we have hope; Jesus, we have your presence in the midst of our betrayal and denial; we have the promise of your empty tomb. You are going ahead of us, walking in the lead! Help us to follow in your footsteps. Cure our residual blindness so that we too can get up and follow you in the way of servanthood and reconciling love. Help us to recognize the areas of resistance in our hearts that still need your healing touch and those aspects of our thinking and acting that have yet to conform to your divine standards. As we reflect now on the path our discipleship should take in this nuclear age, we beg you, turn your loving attention to us as you did to Bartimaeus, and ask us as you did him: "What would you have me do for you?" Having walked with you these weeks, we don't ask for love without risks, but simply: Lord, that we might see! Amen.

LITANY OF REPENTANCE AND HOPE

Jesus calls: "Reform your lives and believe in the gospel!" Faith in Christ requires converting our hearts and our hopes. It means giving testimony of our discipleship in a believing way of seeing, a hopeful way of judging, and a loving way of serving all of God's people in Christ's name. Let us ask the Lord to pardon our failures of trust and fidelity and to set us on the path to life.

RESPONSE: *Lord, lead us to repentance.*

For questioning the authority of Jesus' teachings on the cross, we ask you: **R.**

For placing human standards above divine compassion, we pray: **R.**

For the moral blindness of our nuclear intention, we beg you: **R.**

For trusting in instruments of death to save us rather than in the power of the Living God, we beseech you: **R.**

For our nation's desecration of the earth and environmental destruction resulting from the mining, testing, production, and deployment of nuclear weapons, we pray: **R.**

For betraying Christ's love in the Eucharist by allowing starvation to claim lives daily, we implore you: **R.**

For not fully believing that the risen Christ is alive in our hearts, we plead: **R.**

RESPONSE: *Lord, give us hope.*

That we may become "new wineskins," fitting vessels of God's Spirit, we pray: **R.**

That our world—freed from armaments—may be a safe place to welcome children, we implore: **R.**

That, touched by Christ, we may impart to others a vision of healing, we beg you: **R.**

That fear and selfishness may be converted through earnest and trusting prayer, we ask: **R.**

That we might risk extending to others the love and forgiveness Christ gives us in the Eucharist, we plead: **R.**

That embracing Christ's nonviolent way may lead us to new life, we beseech you: **R.**

THE RISK OF THE CROSS

Mark 16:1–8

When the sabbath was over, Mary Magdalene, Mary, the mother of James, and Salome bought spices so that they might go and anoint him. Very early when the sun had risen, on the first day of the week, they came to the tomb. They were saying to one another, "Who will roll back the stone for us from the entrance to the tomb?" When they looked up, they saw that the stone had been rolled back; it was very large. Entering the tomb they saw a young man sitting on the right side, clothed in a white robe, and they were utterly amazed. He said to them, "Do not be amazed! You seek Jesus of Nazareth, the crucified. He has been raised; he is not here. Behold, the place where they laid him. But go and tell his disciples and Peter, 'He is going before you to Galilee; there you will see him, as he told you.'" Then they went out and fled from the tomb, seized with trembling and bewilderment. They said nothing to anyone, for they were afraid.

Seeing beyond the empty tomb

Carrying perfumed oils, the faithful women make their way to the tomb of Jesus to serve him in death as they did in life. Their grief at the death of a loved one—a death by shameful public execution—is heavy. As they approach the tomb they worry: "Who will roll back the stone for us from the entrance of the tomb?" (16:3).

Who, we ask, will roll back the stone today? Christ is continuously executed in the ultimate death intention, the willingness to use nuclear weapons. The earth itself is becoming Christ's tomb. Who will roll away the stone of vengeance and empty the death threat of its power? The nuclear intention in our hearts and its infernal manifestations in our world are, it seems, too great to lift. For most of us, there is greater assurance in the power of nuclear weapons and military might than in our vulnerable faith in the power of Jesus and his Kingdom. The planetary tomb is becoming more tightly sealed; the cumulative history of human sinfulness increasingly conceals the power that could truly liberate us all. Our fears and hardness of heart seal up the life of Christ within us. We count him among the dead.

When the women look, they discover that the stone has been rolled back. The obstacle was in their mind, in their pessimistic expectation. They look to see a looming impediment, but instead they find something wholly different, the evidence of God's reign at hand. A new expectation comes alive in them as they look upon the empty tomb.

Penetrating faith is needed because the revelation of the power of God's Kingdom at work is deep and mysterious. The empty tomb is the symbol of the resurrection. How paradoxical that emptiness speaks of God! Emptiness awes us and frightens us; it begs for something more. We think of empty missile silos and shudder at the prospect of explosive death. We think of empty grain silos and know that these signify despair for countless millions. Yet empty places often hide within them a seed that will grow unencumbered to fullness. Jesus' self-emptying love in life and death blossoms in fruitfulness from the empty tomb. His risen life conquers the emptiness of death. It is the death threat of Calvary that is hollow, not the promise of new life in Christ.

The rock set in place to guard the dead is a telling symbol of our faithlessness. Our pathetic deterrents designed to wall up our scarcely buried fears are powerless to make us secure. Jesus wants to break open these fetters to free us for a life beyond repressive fear. He invites us to empty ourselves of our paralyzing fear of death, of our need to lord it over others to make our importance felt, and of our desperate fear of being last and least.

Like the women at the tomb, our journey of discipleship will be rewarded when we look "for Jesus of Nazareth, the one who was crucified" (16:6). To have Christian hope requires that the human, vulnerable, forgiving way of Christ becomes our way as well. It is significant that the risen Lord, on the morning of his ultimate vindication, is called by the most human of titles. He is Jesus of Nazareth. The hometown name confirms his status as one of us, as a marginal Galilean. Even in triumph Jesus identifies with the last and the least, and to these he returns as he promised (16:7). Furthermore, Jesus is "the one who was crucified." The cross of Jesus is not forgotten. Easter glory does not erase the wounds of unconditional love. Christ would have us remember both his limitless love and our complicity in the woundedness of our brothers and sisters.

"He has been raised up; he is not here. See the place where they laid him" (16:6). The empty tomb invites us to test our fragile faith. In discovering the empty tomb, we, like the women disciples, become frightened and amazed. Yet as we gaze into the emptiness, we are challenged to believe that Jesus is not among the dead but among the living. To believe that the crucified Nazarene has been raised to life gives us resurrected hearts. Our fears and amazement slowly dissipate, giving way to the profound realization that Jesus is alive. He has forever overcome the cross and the forces of death!

This newfound hope revives our deadened hearts, and our faith is revitalized. We become empowered to journey with Jesus beyond the empty tomb.

Jesus' journey beyond the tomb takes him back to Galilee, the place where his ministry began. It is there, the place of the outcasts and the neglected, to which Jesus returns to continue his mission of servanthood. Jesus journeys ahead of us to this remote place and invites us to join him there. He promises us that if we embark on this pilgrimage of faith, we will *see* him. This promise gives us new hope. In this nuclear age, we can face the challenges before us and be sustained in times of trial. We can fearlessly risk proclaiming with our lives that the way of the cross is the means to true peace and new life. For Jesus, the Lord of Life, has gone ahead of us into the Galilees of our world and will be with us through our most perilous moments. To remind us of his constant guidance and sustenance on our journey, he has given us his Eucharist, the living food that endures forever. The promise of new life awaits us beyond the cross. The challenge is to accept his invitation to discipleship and to journey with him wherever he calls us.

A PSALM OF PEACEMAKING *(Recite together)*

We live in a time of kairos,
   when humanity stands on the border of a promised time,
   when God's people are summoned to obedience and faithfulness
      to preserve God's creation,
      to stand with the poor and oppressed everywhere,
      and to stand together as the people of the earth;

when with confession and with humility we repent
   of our blindness to the division and war in our own hearts
      and in our own land,
   our obsession with money and our pursuit of power,
   our irrational belief in security through weaponry,
   and our worship of secular gods.
We are called
   to be obedient to Jesus Christ, the Prince of Peace,
      who loves the whole world and
      who invites us to be stewards of the earth and servants of his people,
      to be co-workers in the new Creation.
Let us be peacemakers.
Let us be called the children of God,
   speaking boldly with moral conviction to the nation
      and to the world,
   building, with God's grace, a new moral order
      in the world community;
   and acting now for world peace, an enterprise of justice,
      an outcome of love.

(FROM "PEACEMAKING: THE BELIEVERS' CALLING," THE UNITED PRESBYTERIAN CHURCH
IN THE USA, 1980)

OFFERING OF INTENTIONS

Offering our prayers of commitment to be faithful disciples of Christ in the nuclear age.

LORD'S PRAYER

Our Father, who art in heaven, hallowed be thy name; thy kingdom come; thy will be done on earth as it is in heaven. Give us this day our daily bread; and forgive us our trespasses as we forgive those who trespass against us; and lead us not into temptation, but deliver us from evil. For the kingdom, the power, and the glory are yours, now and forever.

Let us express to one another a sign of Christ's peace.

SHARING OF THE EUCHARIST

TAKING THE VOW OF NONVIOLENCE
For those who choose (see pages 113–14).

THE PRAYER OF ST. FRANCIS OF ASSISI

Lord, make me an instrument of thy peace.
    Where there is hatred, let me sow love;
    Where there is injury, pardon;
    Where there is doubt, faith;
    Where there is despair, hope;
    Where there is darkness, light;
  And where there is sadness, joy.

O Divine Master, grant that I may not so much
    Seek to be consoled as to console;
    To be understood as to understand;
    To be loved as to love;
  For it is in giving that we receive,
    It is in pardoning that we are pardoned,
    And it is in dying that we are born to eternal life.

(Although commonly attributed to Francis of Assisi, this prayer cannot be traced back earlier than 1912, when it appeared in the French Magazine, *La Clochette*, with no author's name.

CONCLUDING SONG

The courage to start

THE COURAGE TO START ✠ *Robert C. Aldridge*

Conversion—from being "thing-related" to being "people-centered"—seldom occurs in one cataclysmic flash of enlightenment but rather through a chain reaction of career-shocking, security-threatening experiences: experiences in love of others rather than the abstract morality that has corrupted this country since the first slave was sold.

To those of us of the World War II era, this transformation may be more painful; we have become further embedded in the mire of competition and personal gain. But it's no easy job for the youth of our nation either—many of whom are bathed in relative affluence.

My own questioning started one night several years ago. My oldest daughter and I were discussing campus activities against Dow Chemical, a company producing napalm for use in Vietnam. Our conversation then swung to my work at Lockheed: designing the Poseidon missile with its cluster of individually targeted re-entry vehicles, each carrying a nuclear warhead.

Showing real concern, she explained, "I'm worried, Dad. Pretty soon the demonstrations will be against *your* work."

That moved me because I saw her real worry was tied to a possible split between us over basic values—a split that might put us on opposite sides of the picket line. Of course, I defended my position (which I truly believed at that time) that building deterrent weapons was holding off a hot war until cold-war differences were negotiated. I posed the problem of stopping our production when the Russians have engaged us in an arms race. Her contention was that someone must have the courage to start.

"Someone must have the courage to start." I could not shake that thought, and it troubled me. A good friend of mine once remarked that when a person made him uncomfortable, he found it advantageous to listen. I was more than uncomfortable—I was trapped. To complete my engineering studies, I had worked full time while attending college for five years. Since getting a degree, my advancement had been good—I was at that time leader of a design group for an advanced re-entry system. All my career preparations had been in this field, and I had worked hard. How could Janet, my wife, and I, with ten children, start over? Where do you get that kind of courage?

In spite of the seemingly formidable obstacles, a new consciousness had dawned on me. I became more aware of things happening at work. I noticed that most people did not really exhibit convictions of pursuing humanitarian projects to prevent war. That myth tinged our environment but was neither accepted nor rejected. It just hung there, unchallenged. Patriotic philosophies of defending our country were subordinated to concern for winning contracts or working more overtime.

I observed very little joy within the guarded gates of Lockheed. Only the intellectual side surfaced, and that was strictly along the lines of "me and my project." That attitude, along with tough-line competition for more responsibility, was the general rule. Motivation of people to gather more and more work under their wing amazed me. I finally diagnosed this "empire building" as groping for security—a need to become indispensable. But I knew of very few who actually achieved permanency: a budget cut or administrative reorganization could result in being declared "surplus" or squeezed out of line in the pecking order.

Potential insecurity and ruthless competition, coupled with the lack of personal satisfaction associated with pursuing wholesome tasks, are underlying reasons for the gloomy atmosphere. Constantly hanging over one's head is the negative force of fear. Lacking is the positive reward of seeing one's labor benefit humanity. I did not realize it at the time, but my interior self was changing from the "I-it" to the "I-Thou" attitude—the death knell of an engineering career in the defense industry.

Had I been more alert, I would have recognized harbingers of this human concern shining through my mechanized mentality sooner. A conversation many years ago, shortly after I started work at Lockheed, still lurks in my memory—probably because I realized in my subconscious that it was never completed.

I had engaged one of my colleagues in a philosophical discussion of religion and its meaning in daily life. He asked, "What do you think God wants you to do most of all?" "Just what I am doing," I responded spontaneously, "to help build this missile to protect our country."

He commented that I was fortunate in my conviction and the conversation died. But that dialogue continued to make me think. Was he beginning to struggle within himself? Or was it just a casual question with an offhand response? Whatever, it disturbed me. But I had not yet learned to listen when disturbed.

Gradually, my awareness of surroundings developed into curiosity as patterns unfolded before me. I saw behind-the-scenes activity associated with the daily newscast. I witnessed a task force set up to circumvent what good might come from negotiations to stop the arms race. I saw numerous violations of the test ban treaty when underground nuclear explosions vented into the Nevada atmosphere. Reports I read indicated we couldn't safely negotiate an anti-ballistic-missile freeze because, in addition to being ineffective, our Safeguard system was too expensive and too controversial to be deployed. Finally, when I saw the trend toward greater accuracy and greater warhead yield—a potential shift from the retaliatory deterrent to a first-strike weapon—I became really uneasy. All this undermining of sincerity at the negotiating table was being kept secret from the American people, and the reasons were obvious: bureaucracy and profits. With access to inside knowledge it was not difficult for me to deduce that we had already reached the saturation point of deterrent capability.

A temporary outlet was involvement in the peace movement. As peace information coordinator for the National Association of Laity (NAL), I was exposed to more study and research, and this time it reached international dimensions. I avidly pursued investigation on how American institutions affect underdeveloped countries. New knowledge of how the corporate pattern (in which I had become so deeply enmeshed) was repressing poor people at home and abroad made my complicity more untenable.

So I built bombs as a profession and worked for peace as a hobby—an existence I pursued openly by taking part in all public peace activities. There was a dormant desire that the FBI would find me out and cancel my security clearance. That would make the decision for me, but they never tumbled. During the NAL convention on peace at New York's Fordham University, I was introduced to the assembly as a Lockheed defense worker. Several men approached me afterward to ask questions regarding my conflict of interest, but apparently they weren't Hoover's men as nothing further came of it. My decision of conscience would not be made by default.

Eventually my peace-seeking activities turned in on me. One can only go so far in quest of justice without coming to terms with his own living pattern. In early 1972, Janet and I started planning for the transition. We itemized objectives, areas to investigate, library research, and people with whom we should discuss our plans. These were all outlined as short-term goals—we would schedule ongoing activity after the investigation phase. Our plan proceeded well until events accelerated our decision.

In August of that same year, Janet and I were sent to Honolulu to offer NAL support during the "Hickam Three" trial. The defendants were members of the Catholic Action of Hawaii, an NAL chapter. Attempting to spark consciousness in the people, the accused poured their own blood over top-secret electronic warfare files at Hickam Air Base, intelligence and targeting center for the Indochina air war. Their words during the pouring illustrate their intense motivation:

> *We pour our blood in the name of the God of Love, who lives now in the world in the maimed flesh of suffering people…*
>
> *We pour our blood to signify the responsibility of American citizens for the most terrible atrocities since Nazi Germany's gas chambers…*
>
> *We pour our blood, finally, in the name of the human family under God, a global community created to live in peace, in brotherhood and sisterhood—a community of love which can become fully real only when we are willing to resist the shedding of others' blood by the giving of our own.*

Firsthand contact with people who jeopardized their liberty for the suffering in the world caused me to quickly single out the double standard in my own life. It was then I realized the date for ending my complicity in a program of destruction must be set, and that date must be soon. Prolonging this decision was compromising my human integrity. "Someone must have the courage to start."

The Honolulu experience filled another need I felt necessary at that time. Up until then, all those I knew who had uprooted their lives resisting immorality did not have families. With six children still living at home I could not completely relate to their actions. Now I met a person who furnished a precedent. James W. Douglass—theologian, adviser to bishops during Vatican II, author, university professor, and "Hickam Three" defendant—is a husband and father of a family. Later, while reading Jim's book *Resistance and Contemplation: The Way of Liberation*, I could see where he had also struggled with a concern for his family and solved it. Part of his dialogue with Jesus goes like this:

> *I fear what they can do to me. It is a fear which runs from my seeing it directly, but a fear which I feel identifying itself with all that I have now and would lose—if my fear should be realized, and they should take it all away.*
>
> Take what away?
>
> *Everything I have.*
>
> Like what, for example?
>
> *Well, if you want an inventory: job, home, friends, reputation, a way of life which adds up to a secure existence for my family and myself. I fear much more for my wife and family than I do for myself. I have no right to neglect their needs because of my own feelings of conscience. My first duty is to my wife and family.*
>
> Your wife is as capable as you are of resistance. Women and men resist together in Indochina. It is in America that men feel such unique obligations toward women: pots and pans for the American woman, napalm for the Vietnamese. Let your family—wife, husband and children together—be a family of resistance. Grant them all the dignity of entering the real world, where most families suffer while yours prospers.

Jim's dialogue with Jesus made me ashamed. I had voiced those same fears and asked those same questions, but I hadn't listened well enough to the answers. I had to see someone actually try the road before I could venture on it. We Christians lean too much on precedents that are merely crutches to bolster our weak determination. We must learn to have confidence in our own convictions. Our subjective morality must yield to a contemporary pattern of spiritual activity.

We set the date for January 1973. Immediately after Christmas vacation I would give notice of my resignation. We would start the new year with a new life.

The four days following Christmas were set aside as a period of family contemplation to unify and crystallize our intentions as a family of resistance. We rented a mountain cabin and retired in wilderness seclusion to read and talk. We were trying to center moral teachings and biblical lessons on our family and how we should face the future. We were building spiritual strength to weather the trying times ahead.

On January 2, 1973, I tendered my resignation. We were now past the point of no return. During that last month I discussed my actions with my co-workers. Some agreed with me and would have liked to do the same, but the needs for security were too strong. That singular fear is the main obstacle to moral action. Theologians have developed theologies of liberation and theologies of civil disobedience, but we still need a theology of courage. It must tangibly relate to the working person with a family and be something more than general rules and abstract teaching; it must be brought alive in shops and offices.

So now I am liberated from the military-industrial complex. Our family is still going through the pain of adjustment. After 25 years of homemaking, Janet now works part-time helping children. I am motivated to do freelance writing because I feel there are things I must say. The kids have taken on more responsibility at home and are growing in self-reliance.

The way ahead is still foggy but, as I told my colleague many years ago, I am doing what I think God wants me to do. We are relying on faith—a faith in ourselves and what we believe and a faith that a force is moving us as long as we, in our free will, respond. Life is scary now. I'm beginning to understand what Daniel Berrigan called "the dark night of resistance" and what Thomas Merton meant when he wrote, "Divine light of faith is thick darkness to the soul."

Well, someone must have the courage.

(Reprinted from *Fellowship*, April 1976. Robert Aldridge worked sixteen years as an aerospace engineer for Lockheed Missiles and Space Company. He was group leader responsible for design on the MK 500 MaRV [Maneuvering Re-entry Vehicle], a type of missile with multiple warheads that can be used with extreme accuracy and that has a first-strike military potential. An outspoken critic against nuclear weapons, he has authored several books on US First-Strike Policy and Nonviolence, most recently, *The Goodness Field: A Guidebook for Proactive Nonviolence*. He is a founding member of the Pacific Life Community).

The history of the nuclear age

Nuclear weapons timeline

1940s

AUGUST 1942	Manhattan Project established in US	*The US sets up the Manhattan Project to develop the first nuclear weapon. It eventually employs more than 130,000 people and costs US$2 billion ($25 billion in 2012 dollars).*
16 JULY 1945	US conducts first ever nuclear test	*The US government tests its first nuclear weapon, code-named "Trinity," in New Mexico. Its yield equals 20,000 tonnes of TNT. The date of the test marks the beginning of the nuclear age.*
6 AUGUST 1945	US drops atomic bomb on Hiroshima	*The US detonates a uranium bomb over the Japanese city of Hiroshima, killing more than 140,000 people within months. Many more later die from radiation-related illnesses.*
9 AUGUST 1945	A second bomb is dropped on Nagasaki	*The US explodes a plutonium bomb over Nagasaki. An estimated 74,000 people die by the end of 1945. Little can be done to ease the suffering of the victims who survive the blast.*

24 JANUARY 1946	UN calls for elimination of atomic weapons	*In its first resolution, the UN General Assembly calls for the complete elimination of nuclear weapons and sets up a commission to deal with the problem of the atomic discovery.*
29 AUGUST 1949	Soviet Union tests its first nuclear bomb	*The Soviet Union explodes a nuclear weapon code-named "First Lightning" in Semipalatinsk, Kazakhstan. It becomes the second nation to develop and successfully test a nuclear device.*

1950s

3 OCTOBER 1952	UK tests nuclear weapon in Australia	*The UK conducts its first nuclear test at Montebello Islands off the coast of Western Australia. It later conducts a series of tests at Maralinga and Emu Fields in South Australia.*
1 NOVEMBER 1952	US tests the first hydrogen bomb	*The US raises the stakes in the nuclear arms race by detonating the first hydrogen bomb at Enewetak Atoll in the Marshall Islands. It is 500 times more powerful than the Nagasaki bomb.*
1 MARCH 1954	US conducts massive "Bravo" test	*The US detonates a 17-megaton hydrogen bomb, "Bravo," at Bikini Atoll in the Pacific Ocean, contaminating a Japanese fishing boat, Lucky Dragon, and residents of Rongelap and Utirik.*
9 JULY 1955	Russell–Einstein manifesto issued	*Bertrand Russell, Albert Einstein, and other leading scientists issue a manifesto warning of the dangers of nuclear war and urging all governments to resolve disputes peacefully.*
17 FEBRUARY 1958	UK disarmament campaign formed	*The Campaign for Nuclear Disarmament in the UK holds its first meeting. Its iconic emblem becomes one of the most widely recognized symbols in the world.*

THE RISK OF THE CROSS

| **1 DECEMBER 1959** | Nuclear tests banned in Antarctica | *The Antarctic Treaty opens for signature. It establishes that "any nuclear explosion in Antarctica and the disposal there of radioactive waste material shall be prohibited."* |

1960s

13 FEBRUARY 1960	France tests its first nuclear weapon	*France explodes its first atomic bomb in the Sahara desert. It has a yield of 60–70 kilotons. It later moves its nuclear tests to the South Pacific. These continue up until 1996.*
30 OCTOBER 1961	Largest ever bomb test conducted	*The Soviet Union explodes the most powerful bomb ever: a 58-megaton atmospheric nuclear weapon, nicknamed the "Tsar Bomba," over Novaya Zemlya off northern Russia.*
16–29 OCTOBER 1962	Cuban Missile Crisis occurs	*A tense standoff begins when the US discovers Soviet missiles in Cuba. The US blockades Cuba for 13 days. The crisis brings the US and Soviet Union to the brink of nuclear war.*
5 AUGUST 1963	Partial Test Ban Treaty opens for signature	*A treaty banning nuclear testing in the atmosphere, in outer space, and under water is signed in Moscow, following large demonstrations in Europe and America against nuclear testing.*
16 OCTOBER 1964	China conducts its first nuclear test	*China explodes its first atomic bomb at the Lop Nor testing site in Sinkiang Province. In total, China conducts 23 atmospheric tests and 22 underground tests at the site.*
14 FEBRUARY 1967	Latin America becomes nuclear-free	*A treaty prohibiting nuclear weapons in Latin America, the Treaty of Tlatelolco, is signed in Mexico City. Parties agree not to manufacture, test, or acquire nuclear weapons.*

| **1 JULY 1968** | Non-Proliferation Treaty is signed | *Under the Non-Proliferation Treaty, non-nuclear-weapon states agree never to acquire nuclear weapons, and the nuclear-weapon states make a legal undertaking to disarm.* |

1970s

| **18 MAY 1974** | India conducts first nuclear test | *India conducts an underground nuclear test at Pokhran in the Rajasthan desert, codenamed the "Smiling Buddha." The government falsely claims it is a peaceful nuclear test.* |
| **22 SEPTEMBER 1979** | Nuclear explosion in Indian Ocean | *A nuclear test explosion occurs over the South Indian Ocean off the Cape of Good Hope. It is thought to have been conducted by South Africa with the assistance of Israel.* |

1980s

12 JUNE 1982	A million people rally for disarmament	*One million people gather in New York City's Central Park in support of the Second United Nations Special Session on Disarmament. It is the largest anti-war demonstration in history.*
10 JULY 1985	Rainbow Warrior ship destroyed	*The Greenpeace ship Rainbow Warrior is destroyed in New Zealand on its way to the Mururoa Atoll to protest French nuclear tests. New Zealand later enacts nuclear-free legislation.*
6 AUGUST 1985	South Pacific becomes nuclear-free	*The South Pacific Nuclear-Free Zone Treaty is signed at Rarotonga in the Cook Islands. The treaty prohibits the manufacturing, stationing, or testing of nuclear weapons within the area.*

10 DECEMBER 1985	Anti-nuclear doctors win Nobel	*The International Physicians for the Prevention of Nuclear War receives the Nobel Peace Prize for its efforts to bridge the cold war divide by focusing on the human costs of nuclear war.*
30 SEPTEMBER 1986	Israel's nuclear program revealed	*The* Sunday Times *publishes information supplied by Israeli nuclear technician Mordechai Vanunu, which leads experts to conclude that Israel may have up to 200 nuclear weapons.*
11–12 OCTOBER 1986	US and Soviet leaders discuss abolition	*US President Ronald Reagan and Soviet President Mikhail Gorbachev meet at Reykjavik, Iceland, where they seriously discuss the possibility of achieving nuclear abolition.*
8 DECEMBER 1987	Intermediate-range missiles banned	*The Soviet Union and US sign the Intermediate-Range Nuclear Forces Treaty to eliminate all land-based missiles held by the two states with ranges between 300 and 3,400 miles.*

1990s

10 JULY 1991	South Africa joins Non-Proliferation Treaty	*South Africa accedes to the Non-Proliferation Treaty. The government claims to have made six nuclear weapons and to have dismantled them all.*
15 DECEMBER 1995	Southeast Asia becomes nuclear-free	*The nations of Southeast Asia create a nuclear-weapon-free zone stretching from Burma in the west, the Philippines in the east, Laos and Vietnam in the north, and Indonesia in the south.*
11 APRIL 1996	Africa becomes a nuclear-free zone	*Officials from 43 African nations sign the Treaty of Pelindaba in Egypt, establishing an African nuclear-weapon-free zone and pledging not to build, test, or stockpile nuclear weapons.*

1 JUNE 1996	Ukraine becomes a nuclear-free state	*Ukraine becomes a nuclear-weapon-free state after transferring the last inherited Soviet nuclear warhead to Russia for destruction. Its president calls on other nations to follow its path.*
8 JULY 1996	World Court says nuclear weapons illegal	*The International Court of Justice hands down an advisory opinion in which it found that the threat or use of nuclear weapons would generally be contrary to international law.*
24 SEPTEMBER 1996	Total nuclear test ban is signed	*The Comprehensive Nuclear Test Ban Treaty opens for signatures at the United Nations. China, France, the UK, Russia, and the US all sign the treaty. India says it will not sign the treaty.*
27 NOVEMBER 1996	Belarus removes its last nuclear missile	*Belarus turns its last nuclear missile over to Russia for destruction. It joins Ukraine and Kazakhstan as former Soviet republics that have given up all their nuclear arms.*
MAY 1998	India and Pakistan conduct nuclear tests	*India conducts three underground nuclear tests, its first in 24 years. One is a thermonuclear weapon. Later in May, Pakistan tests six nuclear weapons in response to India's tests.*

2000s

9 OCTOBER 2006	North Korea conducts nuclear test	*The North Korean government announces that it has successfully conducted a nuclear test, becoming the eighth country in the world to do so. It provokes international condemnation.*
30 APRIL 2007	ICAN is launched internationally	*The International Campaign to Abolish Nuclear Weapons is founded in Australia. It calls for the immediate start of negotiations on a treaty to prohibit and eliminate nuclear weapons.*

2010s		
4-5 MARCH 2013	Norway hosts first humanitarian conference	*The Norwegian government hosts the first-ever intergovernmental conference to examine the humanitarian impact of nuclear weapons, bringing together diplomats from 128 states.*
14 FEBRUARY 2014	Mexico conference calls for ban	*The chair of the Second Conference on the Humanitarian Impact of Nuclear Weapons, held in Mexico, concludes that the time has come for a diplomatic process to ban nuclear weapons.*
9 DECEMBER 2014	Austria issues landmark pledge	*As host of the Vienna Conference on the Humanitarian Impact of Nuclear Weapons, Austria issues a landmark pledge to stigmatize, prohibit, and eliminate nuclear weapons.*
27 MARCH 2017	Nuclear ban treaty negotiations begin	*At the United Nations, the overwhelming majority of the world's governments begin negotiations on a treaty to prohibit nuclear weapons, leading toward their total elimination.*
7 JULY 2017	UN adopts nuclear weapon ban treaty	*Following weeks of intensive negotiations, two-thirds of the world's nations vote to adopt the landmark UN Treaty on the Prohibition of Nuclear Weapons.*

SOURCE: INTERNATIONAL COALITION TO ABOLISH NUCLEAR WEAPONS

(WWW.ICANW.ORG/NUCLEAR_WEAPONS_HISTORY)

Notes:

* During 2019 the US withdrew from the Iran Nuclear Deal (JCPOA) and the Intermediate Nuclear Forces (INF) Treaty with Russia.

* As of March 2020, 36 countries have ratified the UN Treaty to Prohibit Nuclear Weapons. When 50 nations ratify the Treaty it will enter into force worldwide, making nuclear weapons illegal under international law.

FEDERATION OF AMERICAN SCIENTISTS RESOURCE ON THE 2018 US NUCLEAR POSTURE REVIEW

The Nuclear Posture Review (NPR) is the Pentagon's primary statement of nuclear policy, produced by the last three presidents in their first years in office. The 2018 NPR perceives a rapidly deteriorating threat environment in which potential nuclear-armed adversaries are increasing their reliance on nuclear weapons. The review reverses decades of bipartisan policy and orders the first new nuclear weapons since the end of the Cold War. Furthermore, the document expands the use of circumstances in which the United States would consider employing nuclear weapons to include "non-nuclear strategic attacks."

The role of US nuclear weapons

The 2018 NPR says US nuclear forces "contribute uniquely to the deterrence of both nuclear and non-nuclear aggression." In addition, the document states they contribute to assuring allies, achieving US objectives if deterrence fails, and hedging "against an uncertain future." The review also raises the possibility of a nuclear strike against any group that "supports or enables terrorist efforts to obtain or employ nuclear devices," extending previous language.

The review also creates a new category of cases in which the US would consider use of nuclear weapons—"significant non-nuclear strategic attacks"—to include attacks on "civilian population or infrastructure." This new category helps serve as justification for "supplements to the planned nuclear force replacement program."

Assumptions about adversaries

Overall, the NPR argues that a range of Russian and Chinese activities have worsened the international threat environment, but it does not fully explain why these activities require increased reliance on nuclear weapons. It states that other nuclear-armed adversaries have failed to follow America's lead in reducing reliance on nuclear weapons. The document concedes that China has not altered its doctrine, while North Korea's capabilities are so rudimentary that "increased reliance" has little meaning.

The nuclear modernization program

The US is engaged in a thirty-year effort to refurbish or replace nearly every warhead and delivery vehicle in the air, sea, and land legs of the nuclear triad. The modernization program was initiated by the Obama Administration. The Trump NPR continues this effort. Instead of making reductions in the Obama plan, the NPR calls for new nuclear weapons and seems to call for retention of the 1.2 megaton B83 nuclear bomb (which had been slated for retirement) with contradictory statements for when the warhead may be retired and what the replacement might be.

New sea-launched cruise missile (SLCM)

The NPR promises to "in the longer term, pursue a modern nuclear-armed SLCM. The document also hopes that the program will help convince Russia to "negotiate seriously a reduction of its non-strategic nuclear weapons" and return to compliance with the INF Treaty. Critical experts believe that a new SLCM would inhibit US forces from carrying out their conventional missions, add little new capability, and be more likely to cause Russian reprisal than compliance.

New low-yield sea-launched ballistic missile (SLBM)

The NPR calls for modifying "a small number of existing SLBM warheads to provide a low-yield option" that "will help counter any mistaken perception of an exploitable 'gap' in US regional deterrence capabilities." The Trump NPR argues that this new capability could provide the option to communicate limited intentions or limit collateral damage. The new capability would blur the distinction between strategic and non-strategic weapons. There is no guarantee that an adversary would understand the strike was limited, whether while in the air or once detonated.

Costs of the arsenal

The NPR document calls the nuclear mission "an affordable priority," noting that "even the highest" of cost projections is "approximately 6.4 percent of the current DoD budget." Yet, Obama Administration officials, military leaders, and federal research agencies have all warned that there is currently no plan to pay what CBO had estimated as the $1.2 trillion (now increased to $1.7 trillion) cost of operating the arsenal over the next thirty years.

Arms control

Overall, the NPR downplays strategic arms control: while stating that the United States "remains willing to engage in a prudent arms control agenda," it adds a new qualification for arms control agreements—that they be "verifiable and enforceable." It is not clear whether any international agreement can be "enforceable." Additionally, the document also states that the government "does not support ratification" of the Comprehensive Test Ban Treaty, which could allow the government to pursue activities incommensurate with the spirit of the treaty.

Source: Federation of American Scientists (www.fas.org)

Chart of Nuclear Arsenals

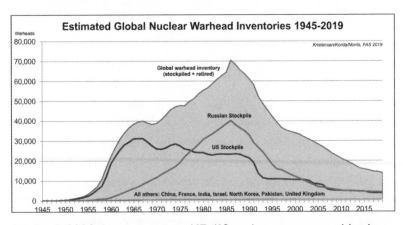

As of early 2020 there an estimated 13,410 nuclear weapons worldwide.
SOURCE: FEDERATION OF AMERICAN SCIENTISTS
https://fas.org/issues/nuclear-weapons/status-world-nuclear-forces/

NEW DOCTRINE FOR JOINT NUCLEAR OPERATIONS

On June 11, 2019, the Pentagon published a new Doctrine for Joint Nuclear Operations. This doctrine, prepared by the Joint Chiefs of Staff, asserts that using nuclear weapons could "create conditions for decisive results and the restoration of strategic stability." "Specifically, the use of a nuclear weapon will fundamentally change the scope of a battle and create conditions that affect how commanders will prevail in conflict." Arms control experts say this marks a shift in US military thinking toward the idea of fighting and winning a nuclear war.

For more information, see: https://fas.org/irp/doddir/dod/jp3_72.pdf.

THE NUCLEAR TESTING TALLY

Since the first nuclear test explosion on July 16, 1945, eight nations have detonated a total of 2,056 nuclear test explosions at dozens of test sites from Lop Nor in China, to the atolls of the Pacific, to Nevada, to Algeria where France conducted its first nuclear device, to western Australia where the UK exploded nuclear weapons, to the South Atlantic, to Semipalatinsk in Kazakhstan, to sites across Russia, and elsewhere.

Most of the test sites are in the lands of indigenous peoples and far from the capitals of the testing governments. A large number of the early tests—528—were detonated in the atmosphere, which spread radioactive materials through the atmosphere. Many underground nuclear blasts have also vented radioactive material into the atmosphere and left radioactive contamination in the soil.

Through nuclear test explosions, the testing nations have been able to proof-test new warhead designs and create increasingly sophisticated nuclear weapons. In 1996, negotiations on a global Comprehensive Test Ban Treaty (CTBT) were concluded, and the treaty was opened for signature on September 24, 1996. The CTBT, which prohibits "any nuclear weapon test explosion or any other nuclear explosion" and established an international test monitoring and verification system, has not yet entered into force. In early 2019 the US conducted a subcritical nuclear that violated the Comprehensive Test Ban Treaty and the Treaty to Prohibit Nuclear Weapons.

A history of nuclear tests and disarmament treaties

Since the first nuclear explosion in July 16, 1945, there have been a total of 2,056 tests conducted by eight nuclear-armed states.

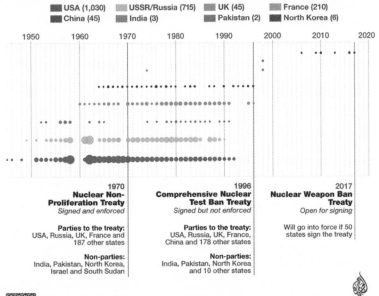

■ USA (1,030) ■ USSR/Russia (715) ■ UK (45) ■ France (210)
■ China (45) ■ India (3) ■ Pakistan (2) ■ North Korea (6)

1970	1996	2017
Nuclear Non-Proliferation Treaty *Signed and enforced*	**Comprehensive Nuclear Test Ban Treaty** *Signed but not enforced*	**Nuclear Weapon Ban Treaty** *Open for signing*
Parties to the treaty: USA, Russia, UK, France and 187 other states	**Parties to the treaty:** USA, Russia, UK, France, China and 178 other states	Will go into force if 50 states sign the treaty
Non-parties: India, Pakistan, North Korea, Israel and South Sudan	**Non-parties:** India, Pakistan, North Korea and 10 other states	

©creativecommons Sources: Arms Control Association, UNODA, CTBTO

@AJLabs ALJAZEERA

NEW GENERATION OF NUCLEAR WEAPONS

US strategic nuclear forces: background, developments, and issues

Even though the United States has reduced the number of warheads deployed on its long-range missiles and bombers, consistent with the terms of the 2010 New START Treaty, it also plans to develop new delivery systems for deployment over the next ten to thirty years. Congress will continue to review these programs, and the funding requested for them, during the annual authorization and appropriations process.

During the Cold War, the US nuclear arsenal contained many types of delivery vehicles for nuclear weapons. The longer-range systems, which included long-range missiles based on US territory, long-range missiles based on submarines, and heavy bombers that could threaten Soviet targets from their bases in the United States, are known as strategic nuclear delivery vehicles. At the end of the Cold War, in 1991, the United States deployed more than 10,000 warheads on these delivery vehicles. With the implementation of New START completed in 2018, the United States is limited to 1,550 accountable warheads on these delivery vehicles, a restriction that will remain in place through early 2021 while the New START Treaty remains in force. The US land-based ballistic missile force (ICBMs) now consists of 400 land-based Minuteman III ICBMs, each deployed with one warhead. This force is consistent with the New START Treaty. The Air Force is also modernizing the Minuteman missiles, replacing and upgrading their rocket motors, guidance systems, and other components, so that they can remain in the force through 2030. It plans to replace the missiles with a new Ground-based Strategic Deterrent around 2029.

The US ballistic missile submarine fleet consists of 14 Trident submarines. Each has been modified to carry 20 Trident II (D-5) missiles—a reduction from 24 missiles per submarine—to meet the launcher limits in the New START Treaty. The Navy converted 4 of the original 18 Trident submarines to carry non-nuclear cruise missiles. Nine of the submarines are deployed in the Pacific Ocean and five are in the Atlantic. The Navy also has undertaken efforts to extend the life of the missiles and warheads so that they and the submarines can remain in the fleet past 2020. It is designing a new submarine that will replace the existing fleet beginning in 2031. The Columbia (SSBN-826) class program is a program to design and build a class of 12 new ballistic missile submarines (SSBNs) to replace the Navy's current force of 14 aging Ohio-class SSBNs. The Navy has identified the Columbia-class program as the Navy's top priority program. The Navy wants to procure the first Columbia-class boat in FY2021.

The US fleet of heavy bombers includes 20 B-2 bombers and 40 nuclear-capable B-52 bombers. This fleet of 60 nuclear-capable aircraft is consistent with the US obligations under New START. The Air Force has also begun to retire the nuclear-armed cruise missiles carried by B-52 bombers, leaving only about half the B-52 fleet equipped to carry nuclear weapons. The Air Force plans to procure both a new long-range bomber and a new "long-range standoff" cruise missile during the 2020s. DOE is also modifying and extending the life of the B61 bomb carried on B-2 bombers and fighter aircraft and the W80 warhead for cruise missiles.

The Trump Administration completed its review of US nuclear forces in February 2018 and reaffirmed the basic contours of the current US force structure and the ongoing modernization programs. The Trump Administration has developed a new low-yield warhead, a version of the W-76 warhead called W76-2, for deployment on Trident II (D-5) missiles. The National Nuclear Security Administration (NNSA) has said the low-yield version, the W76-2, is configured with a yield of less than 10 kilotons. Congress provided the Navy with $19.6 million in the FY2020 budget to begin integrating the warhead into the submarine force. NNSA has not disclosed the total number of planned W76-2 warheads but they are already being deployed.

The United States has actively pursued the development of hypersonic weapons—maneuvering weapons that fly at speeds of at least Mach 5—as a part of its conventional prompt global strike program since the early 2000s. In recent years, the United States has focused such efforts on developing hypersonic glide vehicles, which are launched from a rocket before gliding to a target, and hypersonic cruise missiles, which are powered by high-speed, air-breathing engines during flight.

SOURCE: CONGRESSIONAL RESEARCH SERVICE

Note:
As of March 2020 the Trump Administration has not made any overtures to Russia to extend the new START Treaty. If the US withdraws from the Treaty, a dangerous new arms race could ensue.

NUCLEAR WEAPON PRODUCERS

Modernization can be misleading, especially when it comes to nuclear weapons. Modernizing nuclear weapons is more about maintaining or expanding the ability to murder civilians using an indiscriminate weapon outlawed by international treaty. Every one of the nine nuclear armed countries is spending significant resources investing in new, more usable, and more destabilizing nuclear weapons. In some of these countries, this work is done by private companies. The Don't Bank On The Bomb project reports on companies that invest in, develop, and/or manufacture nuclear weapons, but the lists are not exhaustive. There are numerous other companies involved on a different scale or more indirectly, for example, companies involved in the production of small parts used in the assembly or maintenance of nuclear devices. It is important to note that the total nuclear weapons industry may be much larger.

The companies described are based in France, India, Italy, the Netherlands, the United Kingdom, and the United States. For complete information, see: https://www.dontbankonthebomb.com/nuclear-weapon-producers.

For a map listing all nuclear facilities in the US, see:
https://www.motherjones.com/politics/2011/11/map-nuclear-bombs-power-weapons/

https://www.visualcapitalist.com/cost-and-composition-of-americas-nuclear-weapons-arsenal

THE NUCLEAR CLUB

These nine nations are known to possess nuclear weapons:

- The United States
- Russia
- Great Britain
- France
- China
- India
- Israel
- Pakistan
- The Democratic People's Republic of Korea

Several former republics of the Union of Soviet Socialist Republics turned the nuclear weapons they possessed over to Russia, including Belarus, Kazakhstan, and Ukraine. Iran and Libya negotiated agreements to halt their development of nuclear weapons. President Donald Trump withdrew the US from the multilateral agreement with Iran, which continues to assert it has no plan to develop nuclear weapons.

SOURCE: ARMS CONTROL ASSOCIATION

Since 1950, there have been an estimated thirty-two nuclear weapon accidents, known as "Broken Arrows." A Broken Arrow is defined as an unexpected event involving nuclear weapons that result in the accidental launching, firing, detonating, theft, or loss of the weapon. To date, a number of nuclear weapons have been lost and never recovered. Here is a partial list of such incidents:

1950s

NOVEMBER 10, 1950 | QUEBEC, CANADA

A B-50 jettisoned a Mark 4 bomb over the St. Lawrence River near Riviere-du-Loup, about 300 miles northeast of Montreal. The weapon's high explosive trigger detonated on impact. The explosion scattered nearly 100 pounds (45 kg) of uranium.

MARCH 10, 1956 | EXACT LOCATION UNKNOWN

Carrying two nuclear capsules on a nonstop flight from MacDill Air Force Base near Tampa, Florida, to an overseas base, a B-47 was reported missing. No trace was ever found of the plane.

JULY 27, 1956 | GREAT BRITAIN

A B-47 bomber crashed into a nuclear weapons storage facility at the Lakenheath Air Base in Suffolk, England, during a training exercise. The nuclear weapons storage facility contained three Mark 6 bombs. Preliminary exams by bomb disposal officers said it was a miracle that one Mark 6 with exposed detonators sheared didn't explode. The B-47's crew was killed.

FEBRUARY 5, 1958 | OFF GEORGIA, UNITED STATES

In a simulated combat mission, a B-47 collided with an F-86 near Savannah, Georgia. After attempting to land at Hunter Air Force Base with the nuclear weapon onboard, the weapon was jettisoned over water and the plane landed safely. Subsequent searches failed to locate the weapon.

1960s

While on airborne alert, a B-52 suffered structural failure of its right wing, resulting in the release of two nuclear weapons. One weapon landed safely with little damage. The second fell free and broke apart near the town of Goldsboro, North Carolina. Some of the uranium from that weapon could not be recovered. No radiological contamination was detectable in the area.

JULY 4, 1961 | NORTH SEA
A cooling system failed, contaminating crew members, missiles, and some parts of a K-19 "Hotel"-class Soviet nuclear-powered ballistic missile submarine off Norway. One of the sub's two reactors soared to 800 degrees Celsius and threatened to melt down the reactor's fuel rods. Several fatalities were reported.

DECEMBER 5, 1965 | PACIFIC OCEAN
An A-4E Skyhawk attack aircraft loaded with one B43 nuclear weapon rolled off the deck of the USS Ticonderoga. Pilot, plane, and weapon were never found.

JANUARY 17, 1966 | PALOMARES, SPAIN
A B-52 carrying four nuclear weapons collided with a KC-135 during refueling operations and crashed near Palomares, Spain. Two weapons were safely recovered after extensive search and recovery efforts. The other two weapons hit land, resulting in detonation of their high explosives and the subsequent release of radioactive materials. Over 1,400 tons of soil was sent to an approved storage site.

APRIL 11, 1968 | PACIFIC OCEAN
A Soviet diesel-powered "Golf"-class ballistic missile submarine sank about 750 miles northwest of the island of Oahu, Hawaii. Reports say the submarine was carrying three nuclear-armed ballistic missiles, as well as several nuclear torpedoes. Part of the submarine was reportedly raised using the CIA's "Glomar Explorer" deep-water salvage ship.

NOVEMBER 1969 | WHITE SEA

The US nuclear-powered submarine Gato reportedly collided with a Soviet submarine on November 14 or 15, 1969, near the entrance of the White Sea.

1980s

OCTOBER 3, 1986 | ATLANTIC OCEAN

A Soviet "Yankee I"-class nuclear-powered ballistic missile submarine suffered an explosion and fire in one of its missile tubes 480 miles east of Bermuda. The submarine sank while under tow on October 6 in 18,000 feet of water. Two nuclear reactors and approximately thirty-four nuclear weapons were on board.

APRIL 7, 1989 | ATLANTIC OCEAN

About 300 miles north of the Norwegian coast, the Komsomolets, a Soviet nuclear-powered attack submarine, caught fire and sank. The vessel's nuclear reactor, two nuclear-armed torpedoes, and forty-two of the sixty-nine crew members were lost.

AUGUST 10, 1985 | NEAR VLADIVOSTOK, RUSSIA

While at the Chazhma Bay repair facility, about thirty-five miles from Vladivostok, an "Echo"-class Soviet nuclear-powered submarine suffered a reactor explosion. The explosion released a cloud of radioactivity that did not reach the city. Ten officers were killed in the explosion.

1990s

FEBRUARY 11, 1992 | BARENTS SEA

A CIS (Commonwealth of Independent States) "Sierra"-class nuclear-powered attack submarine collided with the US nuclear-powered attack submarine Baton Rouge. Both vessels reportedly suffered only minor damage.

SOURCES: US DEFENSE DEPARTMENT; CAMPAIGN FOR NUCLEAR DISARMAMENT; NATIONAL SECURITY ARCHIVE; GREENPEACE; JOSHUA HANDLER, PRINCETON UNIVERSITY; UNITED PRESS INTERNATIONAL; THE ASSOCIATED PRESS; *BLIND MAN'S BLUFF: THE UNTOLD STORY OF AMERICAN SUBMARINE ESPIONAGE*

PARTIAL LISTING OF INCIDENTS OF US THREATS TO USE NUCLEAR WEAPONS AS NUCLEAR BLACKMAIL

The United States is the only country to have used the atomic bomb. Since the A-bombings of Hiroshima and Nagasaki, US presidents have threatened nuclear war to bolster US imperial ambitions. Also, the US has refused to adopt a no first-use policy and declaring it "reserves the right to use" nuclear weapons first in the case of conflict. In *Empire and the Bomb: How the US Uses Nuclear Weapons to Dominate the World* (Pluto Press, 2007), Dr. Joseph Gerson, author, nuclear specialist, and peace campaigner, reveals that the US made more than twenty threats of nuclear attack during the Cold War—against Russia, China, Vietnam, and the Middle East. He details how such threats continued through 2006 under Presidents George H.W. Bush, Bill Clinton, and George W. Bush.

1946 — Truman threatens Soviets regarding northern Iran.

1946 — Truman sends SAC bombers to intimidate Yugoslavia following the downing of a US aircraft over Yugoslavia.

1948 — Truman threatens Soviets in response to Berlin blockade.

1950 — Truman threatens the Chinese when US Marines are surrounded at Chosin Reservoir in Korea.

1951 — Truman approves a military request to attack Manchuria with nuclear weapons if significant numbers of new Chinese forces enter the war.

1953 — Eisenhower threatens China to force an end to the Korean War on terms acceptable to the US.

1954 — Eisenhower's Secretary of State John Foster Dulles offers the French three tactical nuclear weapons to break the siege at Dien Bien Phu, Vietnam.

1954 — Eisenhower uses nuclear-armed SAC bombers to reinforce a CIA backed coup in Guatemala.

1956 — Nikolai Bulganin threatens London and Paris with nuclear attacks, demanding withdrawal from Egypt. Eisenhower counters by threatening the USSR while also demanding that the British and French withdraw from Egypt.

1958 — Eisenhower orders the Joint Chiefs of Staff to prepare to use nuclear weapons against Iraq if necessary, to prevent extension of revolution into Kuwait.

1958 — Eisenhower orders the Joint Chiefs of Staff to prepare to use nuclear weapons against China if they invade the island of Quemoy.

1961 — Kennedy threatens Soviets during the Berlin Crisis.

1962 — Cuban Missile Crisis.

1967 — Johnson threatens Soviets during the Middle East War.

1967 — Johnson threatens nuclear attack to break the siege at Khe Sanh.

1969 — Nixon's "November ultimatum" against Vietnam.

1970 — Nixon signals US preparations to fight a nuclear war during the Black September War in Jordan.

1973 — Kissinger threatens the Soviet Union during the last hours of the "October War" in the Middle East.

1973 — Nixon pledges to South Vietnamese President Thieu that he will respond with nuclear attacks or the bombing of North Vietnam's dikes if it violates the provisions of the Paris Accords.

1975 — Secretary of Defense Schlesinger threatens N. Korea with nuclear retaliation should it attack S. Korea following the US defeat in Vietnam.

1980 — The Carter Doctrine declares US commitment to use "any means necessary" to maintain Middle East dominance. Presidential Directive 59 is announced moving US nuclear war-fighting doctrine from mutual assured destruction to "flexible" and more "limited" nuclear war fighting.

1981 — Reagan affirms the Carter Doctrine.

1990–1991 — Bush threatens Iraq during the Gulf War.

1993–1994 — Clinton threatens and confronts N. Korea.

1996 — Clinton threatens Libya with nuclear attack to prevent completion of an underground chemical weapons production plant.

1998 — Clinton threatens Iraq with nuclear attack.

2001 — Secretary of Defense Donald Rumsfeld refuses to rule out using tactical nuclear weapons against Afghan caves believed to shelter Osama Bin Laden.

2002 — Bush communicates an implied threat to counter any Iraqi use of chemical or biological weapons with a nuclear attack.

2003 — US mobilization and implicit nuclear threats against N. Korea.

2006 — Implicit US threats to bomb Iran's nuclear infrastructure with "bunker buster" atomic bombs.

Note:

President Trump has threatened to use nuclear weapons on several occasions, including in 2017 against North Korea, and in 2019 against Iran.

US NUCLEAR WEAPONS STOCKPILE—JANUARY 2020

The Defense Department maintains an estimated stockpile of approximately 3,800 warheads. Of these, only 1,750 warheads are deployed, while approximately 2,050 are held in reserve. Additionally, approximately 2,000 retired warheads are awaiting dismantlement, giving a total inventory of approximately 5,800 nuclear warheads. Of the 1,750 warheads that are deployed, 400 are on land-based intercontinental ballistic missiles, roughly 900 are on submarine-launched ballistic missiles, 300 are at bomber bases in the US, and 150 (possibly 100) B61 gravity bombs are deployed at six different bases in the Netherlands, Belgium, Germany, Italy, and Turkey.

SOURCE: FAS-HTTPS://FAS.ORG./ISSUES/NUCLEAR-WEAPONS/NUCLEAR-NOTEBOOK/

Gar Alperowitz, *Atomic Diplomacy: Hiroshima and Potsdam; The Use of the Atomic Bomb and the American Confrontation with Soviet Power*. Viking/Penguin, 1985. Provides important new evidence to support the thesis that the primary reason for using the bomb was not to end the war in Japan, as was said at the time, but to "make the Russians more manageable."

Daniel Ellsberg, *The Doomsday Machine: Confessions of a Nuclear War Planner*. Bloomsbury USA, 2017. A comprehensive, revealing look at US nuclear war planning and procedures from a military analyst turned renowned peacemaker.

Dan Zak, *Almighty: Courage, Resistance, and Existential Peril in the Nuclear Age*. Blue Rider Press, 2016. Tells the story of the Transform Now Plowshares in the context of the perilous history of the Nuclear Age, examines key security concerns, and reshapes the accepted narratives surrounding nuclear weapons.

Eric Schlosser, *Command and Control: Nuclear Weapons, the Damascus Accident and the Illusion of Safety*. Penguin Press, 2013. Presents a detailed look at the state of nuclear weapons security and the problems presented by mere possession of these weapons.

William Greider, *Fortress America: The American Military and the Consequences of Peace*. Public Affairs Books, 1998. Useful background— how the military-industrial complex works.

Richard Rhodes, *The Making of the Atomic Bomb*. Simon and Schuster, 2012. A detailed history of the race to develop nuclear weapons during World War II. Together with two of his other books, *Dark Sun: The Making of the Hydrogen Bomb* and *Arsenals of Folly: The Making of the Nuclear Arms Race*, Rhodes has written a comprehensive history of nuclear weapons and the nuclear arms race.

Timmon Milne Wallis, *Disarming the Nuclear Argument*. Luath Press, 2017. A powerful text that dispels myths and wishful thinking about nuclear deterrence and nuclear arsenals.

The Church on war and peace

CHRISTIAN PACIFISM ✠ *Joseph Fahey*

Much can be learned from the history of Christian pacifism in the quest for a human world order. Indeed, one might be so bold as to say that the pacifist experience of Christianity has never been so relevant as in our own century in which we must make a literally life-or-death decision concerning the human species. Martin Luther King's insight that today "the choice is between nonviolence or nonexistence" is neither utopian nor optimistic—it is the product of a sober realism that tells us that we simply cannot continue on our present course.

It is time to challenge those who pursue the arms race to be "realistic." Their naive assumption that a "balance of terror" will lead to a steady peace is backed neither by the tenets of morality, the basics of logic, nor the facts of history. Let us learn, then, from that Christian minority who chose life over death, nonviolence over violence, and resistance over submission.

In order to understand the long history of Christian pacifism one must, of course, examine the nonviolence of Jesus. It is quite clear that Jesus inherited the prophetic mandate for social justice and nonviolent reconciliation of enemies. He came to help "the blind see, the lame walk, the lepers [to be] cleansed, the deaf hear, the dead rise, the poor [to] have the gospel preached to them" (Matthew 11:4–6). While Jesus' work was described principally in terms of justice (social justice, that is, since a completely individualistic ethic is impossible when talking about the needs of others), its method was the pursuit of nonviolence.

In the Sermon on the Mount Jesus blessed the peacemakers and said they should be called children of God (Mt 5:9). He likewise counseled his followers, "You have heard the commandment, 'You shall love your countryman but hate your enemy.' My command to you is: love your enemies, pray for your persecutors. This will prove you are children of your heavenly Father" (Mt 5:43–45).

In one of his very last statements Jesus warned us that those who use the sword (violence) will perish by the sword (Mt 26:54). He thus fulfilled his mission to be the Suffering Servant of God who would bring justice to his people by dying for them.

These passages present the main thrust of Jesus' attitude toward nonviolence. While isolated passages from the gospels have been used by some to justify violence, they have not swayed the opinions of contemporary Scripture scholars. In addition, these same scholars tell us that Jesus was put to death because of the social and political implications of his work. He was murdered by the Romans as if he were a revolutionary Zealot who threatened the established imperial order. Jesus' message was one of social justice and nonviolence—it attacked the very roots of the unjust and violent society in which he lived. He was, in essence, seeking to form a new global culture based on the priority of human needs and nonviolent love.

It is well known that for at least three centuries the early Christians followed the pacifist example of Jesus. They were forbidden to kill enemies or join the army, and even those in the army had to resign when they were converted.

Four arguments are normally offered to explain the pacifism of early Christianity: the imminent Eschaton, aversion to Rome, idolatry, and the incompatibility between *agape* and war. One can conclude, however, that only the last reason was universally approved by the early Fathers of the Church and Christians in general. This was because the Christian word for love—*agape*—meant selfless concern for others, even one's enemies. It was thus inconceivable to the early Christians that one could fulfill Jesus' command to love one's enemy while at the same time preparing to kill that person.

Clearly, the early Christians believed that because they were followers of Jesus they could not kill. The following quotes are representative:

Christ in disarming Peter ungirt every soldier. TERTULLIAN

It is not right for us either to see or hear a man being killed. MINUCIUS FELIX

God did not deem it becoming to his own divine legislation to allow the killing of any man whatsoever. ORIGEN

We who were filed with war and mutual slaughter and every wickedness have each of us in all the world changed our weapons of war... swords into plows and spears into agricultural instruments....We who formerly murdered one another now not only do not lie or deceive our judges, we gladly die confessing Christ. JUSTIN MARTYR

In AD 295 a North African named Maximilian was beheaded because he refused to serve in the Roman army. He believed that Christians must conscientiously refuse military service. During his trial he stated: "My arms are with the Lord. I cannot fight for any earthly consideration. I am now a Christian... and it is unlawful to do evil."

The early Christians saw themselves as global citizens whose mission was to continue the witness of Jesus in "comforting the afflicted and afflicting the comfortable" by being pacifists (peacemakers) in his name. One could argue that the Christian community was never so strong as when it was weak and never so powerful as when it was powerless. We must remember that the nonviolent witness of the early Christians conquered the most powerful empire then existent in the world. Those who argue that, from a historical viewpoint, nonviolence has not worked must explain how Christians overcame the Roman Empire without armies or violence.

But, alas, the victory was not permanent, for by the fourth and fifth centuries thinkers such as Ambrose and Augustine had abandoned any hope for the Kingdom in this life and had come to accept the doctrine of the "just war." There is strong evidence to indicate that a major reason why many Christians accepted the use of violence to defend the Roman Empire was the growing fusion between Rome and Christianity. Many came to believe that the *Pax Christiana* and the *Pax Romana* were joint works of God.

This fusion between Christianity and nationalism led to the acceptance of violence as an instrument of national (Christian) policy. The Church has never been the same since. The "just war" in the fifth century led to the Crusades in the eleventh century. By that time nonviolence not only was not accepted by the Christian leadership but was considered sinful and a sign of weakness.

But pacifism has always survived in Christianity. Religious orders of men and women carefully preserve the nonviolent witness of the early Church. People such as Benedict (d. 547, Italy), Francis (1182?–1226, Italy), Clare (1193?–1253, Italy), Ignatius Loyola (1491–1556, Spain), Erasmus (1466–1536, Holland), Thomas More (1478–1535, England), and the numerous orders of religious women have given us an unending witness of nonviolent service which would take volumes to fill. We owe them much.

The Protestant churches have given no less dramatic testimony. The most outstanding witnesses have been the Quakers, the Anabaptists (now the Mennonites and the Hutterites), and the Brethren. These people have often influenced society in far greater proportion than their numbers and persevered in pacifism through persecution, war, and social rejection.

In our own time a remarkable phenomenon seems to be taking place. Almost all Christian churches seem to be returning (in various degrees) to the pacifism of early Christianity. Undoubtedly, new biblical and theological scholarship is spurring this movement. In addition, however, many are coming to realize that unless we adopt a more pacifist witness we simply will not survive. In short, be it from practical necessity or from biblical and historical insight, many more Christians are coming to see war and violence, including institutional violence, as the central blasphemy of our age.

We are called to be one race—a human race—and are challenged to create a truly human world order. It is within our power, but is it within our vision? The discovery of the long history of Christian pacifism should remind us that so many others have not lost that vision. We are spiritual descendants of parents who have longed for a truly human word. We cannot fail them.

(Joseph J. Fahey, Ph.D., is former professor of religious studies and director of the Peace Studies Institute at Manhattan College and is the author of several books, including *War and the Christian Conscience*.)

DENOMINATIONAL STATEMENTS
ON PEACE AND NUCLEAR DISARMAMENT

(Statements from the listed denominations and other faith traditions and interreligious bodies can be found at the website of the Friends Committee on National Legislation: www.fcnl.org/updates/faith-statements-on-nuclear-disarmament-155.)

American Baptist Church
Church of the Brethren
Episcopal Church
Evangelical Lutheran Church in America
Mennonite Church USA
National Association of Evangelicals
Presbyterian Church (USA)
The Religious Society of Friends (Quakers)
Unitarian Universalist Association
United Church of Christ
United Methodist Church

Presbyterian Church Statement on Nuclear Weapons, June 20, 2018
(https://www.presbyterianmission.org/story/nuclear-disarmament-renewing-hope-against-all-odds/)

VATICAN AND PAPAL STATEMENTS ON NUCLEAR WEAPONS

Catholic Church

USCCB statements are here: http://usccb.org/issues-and-action/human-life-and-dignity/war-and-peace/nuclear-weapons/index.cfm. Vatican and papal statements are excerpted below. For more, see: www.vatican.va.

Every act of war directed to the indiscriminate destruction of whole cities or vast areas with their inhabitants is a crime against God and man, which merits firm and unequivocal condemnation. (Vatican Council II, *Gaudium et Spes*, no. 80)

From Pope Francis, World Day of Peace 2017
Nonviolence: A Style of Politics for Peace (excerpts)

A BROKEN WORLD

2. While the last century knew the devastation of two deadly World Wars, the threat of nuclear war and a great number of other conflicts, today, sadly, we find ourselves engaged in a horrifying world war fought piecemeal. It is not easy to know if our world is presently more or less violent than in the past, or to know whether modern means of communications and greater mobility have made us more aware of violence, or, on the other hand, increasingly inured to it.

In any case, we know that this "piecemeal" violence, of different kinds and levels, causes great suffering: wars in different countries and continents; terrorism, organized crime, and unforeseen acts of violence; the abuses suffered by migrants and victims of human trafficking; and the devastation of the environment. Where does this lead? Can violence achieve any goal of lasting value? Or does it merely lead to retaliation and a cycle of deadly conflicts that benefit only a few "warlords"?

Violence is not the cure for our broken world. Countering violence with violence leads at best to forced migrations and enormous suffering, because vast amounts of resources are diverted to military ends and away from the everyday needs of young people, families experiencing hardship, the elderly, the infirm, and the great majority of people in our world. At worst, it can lead to the death, physical and spiritual, of many people, if not of all.

THE GOOD NEWS

3. Jesus himself lived in violent times. Yet he taught that the true battlefield, where violence and peace meet, is the human heart: for "it is from within, from the human heart, that evil intentions come" (Mk 7:21). But Christ's message in this regard offers a radically positive approach. He unfailingly

preached God's unconditional love, which welcomes and forgives. He taught his disciples to love their enemies (cf. Mt 5:44) and to turn the other cheek (cf. Mt 5:39). When he stopped her accusers from stoning the woman caught in adultery (cf. Jn 8:1–11), and when, on the night before he died, he told Peter to put away his sword (cf. Mt 26:52), Jesus marked out the path of nonviolence. He walked that path to the very end, to the cross, whereby he became our peace and put an end to hostility (cf. Eph 2:14–16). Whoever accepts the Good News of Jesus is able to acknowledge the violence within and be healed by God's mercy, becoming in turn an instrument of reconciliation. In the words of Saint Francis of Assisi: "As you announce peace with your mouth, make sure that you have greater peace in your hearts."

To be true followers of Jesus today also includes embracing his teaching about nonviolence.

MORE POWERFUL THAN VIOLENCE

4. Nonviolence is sometimes taken to mean surrender, lack of involvement and passivity, but this is not the case. When Mother Teresa received the Nobel Peace Prize in 1979, she clearly stated her own message of active nonviolence: "We in our family don't need bombs and guns, to destroy to bring peace—just get together, love one another… and we will be able to overcome all the evil that is in the world." For the force of arms is deceptive. "While weapons traffickers do their work, there are poor peacemakers who give their lives to help one person, then another and another and another"; for such peacemakers, Mother Teresa is "a symbol, an icon of our times."

The decisive and consistent practice of nonviolence has produced impressive results. The achievements of Mahatma Gandhi and Khan Abdul Ghaffar Khan in the liberation of India and of Dr. Martin Luther King Jr. in combating racial discrimination will never be forgotten. Women in particular are often leaders of nonviolence, as, for example, was Leymah Gbowee and the thousands of Liberian women, who organized pray-ins and nonviolent protest that resulted in high-level peace talks to end the second civil war in Liberia.

The Church has been involved in nonviolent peace-building strategies in many countries, engaging even the most violent parties in efforts to build a just and lasting peace.

Such efforts on behalf of the victims of injustice and violence are not the legacy of the Catholic Church alone, but are typical of many religious traditions, for which "compassion and nonviolence are essential elements pointing to the way of life." I emphatically reaffirm that "no religion is terrorist." Violence profanes the name of God. Let us never tire of repeating: "The name of God cannot be used to justify violence. Peace alone is holy. Peace alone is holy, not war!"

THE DOMESTIC ROOTS OF A POLITICS OF NONVIOLENCE

5. If violence has its source in the human heart, then it is fundamental that nonviolence be practiced before all else within families. An ethics of fraternity and peaceful coexistence between individuals and among peoples cannot be based on the logic of fear, violence, and closed-mindedness, but on responsibility, respect, and sincere dialogue. Hence, I plead for disarmament and for the prohibition and abolition of nuclear weapons: nuclear deterrence and the threat of mutual assured destruction are incapable of grounding such an ethics. I plead with equal urgency for an end to domestic violence and to the abuse of women and children.

MY INVITATION

6. Peacebuilding through active nonviolence is the natural and necessary complement to the Church's continuing efforts to limit the use of force by the application of moral norms; she does so by her participation in the work of international institutions and through the competent contribution made by so many Christians to the drafting of legislation at all levels. Jesus himself offers a "manual" for this strategy of peacemaking in the Sermon on the Mount. The eight Beatitudes (cf. Mt 5:3–10) provide a portrait of the person we could describe as blessed, good, and authentic. Blessed are the meek, Jesus tells us, the merciful and the peacemakers, those who are pure in heart, and those who hunger and thirst for justice.

I pledge the assistance of the Church in every effort to build peace through active and creative nonviolence. On 1 January 2017, the new Dicastery for Promoting Integral Human Development will begin its work. It will help the Church to promote in an ever more effective way "the inestimable goods of justice, peace, and the care of creation" and concern for "migrants, those in need, the sick, the excluded and marginalized, the imprisoned and the unemployed, as well as victims of armed conflict, natural disasters, and all forms of slavery and torture." Every such response, however modest, helps to build a world free of violence, the first step toward justice and peace.

IN CONCLUSION

7. "All of us want peace. Many people build it day by day through small gestures and acts; many of them are suffering, yet patiently persevere in their efforts to be peacemakers." In 2017, may we dedicate ourselves prayerfully and actively to banishing violence from our hearts, words, and deeds, and to becoming nonviolent people and to building nonviolent communities that care for our common home. "Nothing is impossible if we turn to God in prayer. Everyone can be an artisan of peace."

Full text: http://www.vatican.va/content/francesco/en/messages/peace/documents/
papa-francesco_20161208_messaggio-l-giornata-mondiale-pace-2017.html

Message from Pope Francis to the UN Conference to Prohibit Nuclear Weapons, March 23, 2017 (Excerpts)

But why give ourselves this demanding and forward-looking goal in the present international context characterized by an unstable climate of conflict, which is both cause and indication of the difficulties encountered in advancing and strengthening the process of nuclear disarmament and nuclear non-proliferation?

If we take into consideration the principal threats to peace and security with their many dimensions in this multipolar world of the twenty-first century, not a few doubts arise regarding the inadequacy of nuclear deterrence as an effective response to such challenges. These concerns are even greater when we consider the catastrophic humanitarian and environmental consequences that would follow from any use of nuclear weapons. Similar cause for concern arises when examining the waste of resources spent on nuclear issues for military purposes, which could instead be used for worthy priorities like the promotion of peace and integral human development. We need also to ask ourselves how sustainable is a stability based on fear, when it actually increases fear and undermines relationships of trust between peoples.

In this context, the ultimate goal of the total elimination of nuclear weapons becomes both a challenge and a moral and humanitarian imperative.

Full text: http://www.vatican.va/content/francesco/en/messages/pont-messages/2017/ documents/papa-francesco_20170323_messaggio-onu.html

Pope Francis Addressing Participants in the International Symposium "Prospects for a World Free of Nuclear Weapons and for Integral Disarmament," November 2017 (Excerpts)

Indeed, the escalation of the arms race continues unabated and the price of modernizing and developing weaponry, not only nuclear weapons, represents a considerable expense for nations. As a result, the real priorities facing our human family, such as the fight against poverty, the promotion of peace, the undertaking of educational, ecological, and healthcare projects, and the development of human rights, are relegated to second place.

Nor can we fail to be genuinely concerned by the catastrophic humanitarian and environmental effects of any employment of nuclear devices. *If we also take into account the risk of an accidental detonation as a result of error of any kind, the threat of their use, as well as their very possession, is to be firmly condemned.* For they exist in the service of a mentality of fear that affects not only the parties in conflict but the entire human race.

International relations cannot be held captive to military force, mutual intimidation, and the parading of stockpiles of arms. Weapons of mass destruction, particularly nuclear weapons, create nothing but a false sense of security. They cannot constitute the basis for peaceful coexistence between members of the human family, which must rather be inspired by an ethics of solidarity.

Full text: http://www.vatican.va/content/francesco/en/speeches/2017/november/documents/ papa-francesco_20171110_convegno-disarmointegrale.html

Address of Pope Francis, Peace Memorial (Hiroshima) November 24, 2019 (Excerpts)

God of mercy and Lord of history, to you we lift up our eyes from this place, where death and life have met, loss and rebirth, suffering and compassion.

Here, in an incandescent burst of lightning and fire, so many men and women, so many dreams and hopes, disappeared, leaving behind only shadows and silence. In barely an instant, everything was devoured by a black hole of destruction and death. From that abyss of silence, we continue even today to hear the cries of those who are no longer. They came from different places, had different names, and some spoke different languages. Yet all were united in the same fate, in a terrifying hour that left its mark forever not only on the history of this country, but on the face of humanity.

Here I pay homage to all the victims, and I bow before the strength and dignity of those who, having survived those first moments, for years afterward bore in the flesh immense suffering, and in their spirit seeds of death that drained their vital energy.

I felt a duty to come here as a pilgrim of peace, to stand in silent prayer, to recall the innocent victims of such violence, and to bear in my heart the prayers and yearnings of the men and women of our time, especially the young, who long for peace, who work for peace, and who sacrifice themselves for peace. I have come to this place of memory and of hope for the future, bringing with me the cry of the poor, who are always the most helpless victims of hatred and conflict.

It is my humble desire to be the voice of the voiceless, who witness with concern and anguish the growing tensions of our own time: the unacceptable inequalities and injustices that threaten human coexistence, the grave inability to care for our common home, and the constant outbreak of armed conflict, as if these could guarantee a future of peace.

With deep conviction I wish once more to declare that the use of atomic energy for purposes of war is today, more than ever, a crime not only against the dignity of human beings but against any possible future for our common home. *The use of atomic energy for purposes of war is immoral, just as the possessing of nuclear weapons is immoral*, as I already said two years ago. We will be judged on this. Future generations will rise to condemn our failure if we spoke of peace but did not act to bring it about among the peoples of the earth. How can we speak of peace even as we build terrifying new weapons of war? How can we speak about peace even as we justify illegitimate actions by speeches filled with discrimination and hate? …

Indeed, if we really want to build a more just and secure society, we must let the weapons fall from our hands. "No one can love with offensive weapons in their hands" (Saint Paul VI, *United Nations Address*, 4 October 1965, 10). When we yield to the logic of arms and distance ourselves from the practice of dialogue, we forget to our detriment that, even before causing victims and ruination, weapons can create nightmares; "they call for enormous expenses, interrupt projects of solidarity and of useful labor, and warp the outlook of nations" (*ibid*). How can we propose peace if we constantly invoke the threat of nuclear war as a legitimate recourse for the resolution of conflicts? May the abyss of pain endured here remind us of boundaries that must never be crossed. A true peace can only be an unarmed peace….

To remember, to journey together, to protect. These are three moral imperatives that here in Hiroshima assume even more powerful and universal significance, and can open a path to peace. For this reason, we cannot allow present and future generations to lose the memory of what happened here. It is a memory that ensures and encourages the building of a more fair and fraternal future; an expansive memory, capable of awakening the consciences of all men and women, especially those who today play a crucial role in the destiny of the nations; a living memory that helps us say in every generation: never again! …

In a single plea to God and to all men and women of good will, on behalf of all the victims of atomic bombings and experiments, and of all conflicts, let us together cry out from our hearts: Never again war, never again the clash of arms, never again so much suffering! May peace come in our time and to our world."

Full Text: http://www.vatican.va/content/francesco/en/messages/pont-messages/2019/
documents/papa-francesco_20191124_messaggio-incontropace-hiroshima.html

PERSONAL STATEMENTS ON PEACE
AND NUCLEAR DISARMAMENT

Albert Einstein

On the day the bomb was dropped on Hiroshima, on that day the American people assumed responsibility before the eyes of the world for the release of the most revolutionary force since the discovery of fire. Each of us, whether as scientists who made the bomb possible and/or as citizens of the nations that applied the knowledge, stands accountable for the use we made and make of this tremendous new force. To our generation has come the possibility of making the most fateful decision in the recorded history of the human race. I believe that human beings capable of restraint, reason, and courage will choose the path of peace. Each of us has it in our power today to act for peace. (First Commemoration of the Bombing of Hiroshima, August 6, 1946)

Mohandas K. Gandhi

I regard the employment of the atomic bomb for the wholesale destruction of men, women, and children as the most diabolical use of science. Nonviolence is the only thing the atomic bomb cannot destroy....Unless now the world adopts nonviolence, it will spell certain suicide for humanity. (From *Nonviolence in Peace and War*, Mohandas K. Gandhi)

Dorothy Day

All our talks about peace and the weapons of the spirit are meaningless unless we try in every way to embrace voluntary poverty and not work in any position, any job, that contributes to war, nor to take any job whose pay comes from the fear of war, of the atomic bomb. (From *On Pilgrimage*)

Love is not the starving of whole populations. Love is not the bombardment of open cities. Love is not killing, it is the laying down of one's life for one's friends. (From *Selected Writings*, Dorothy Day)

Martin Luther King Jr.

If we assume that humankind has a right to survive then we must find an alternative to war and destruction. In a day when sputniks dash through outer space and guided ballistic missiles are carving highways of death through the stratosphere, nobody can win a war. The choice today is no longer between violence and nonviolence. It is either nonviolence or nonexistence.

I am convinced that the Church cannot remain silent while humankind faces the threat of being plunged into the abyss of nuclear annihilation. If the Church is to remain true to its mission it must call for an end to the arms race. ("Pilgrimage to Nonviolence" from *Strength to Love*. In 1957, Dr. King publicly expressed his opposition to nuclear weapons in *Ebony* Magazine.)

Sarah Hutchinson (Cherokee teacher)

A thousand years ago the young men buried their fathers; during wartime the fathers buried the young men; now with nuclear technology we are burying the children of the future.

Daniel Berrigan, SJ

Our plight is very primitive from a Christian point of view. We are back where we started. Thou shalt not kill. Everything today comes down to that—everything. (*The Catholic Worker*, December 2001)

Archbishop Raymond Hunthausen

We need to find our way back to the way of nonviolence...which Jesus calls us to in the Gospel and on the cross....God calls us to name the evil our society has embraced so wholeheartedly in our nuclear arms, and to do so clearly. Trident is the Auschwitz of Puget Sound because of the massive cooperation required in our area—the enormous sinful complicity that is necessary—for the eventual incineration of millions of our brother and sister human beings. I say with deep sorrow that our nuclear war preparations are the global crucifixion of Jesus....Our nuclear weapons are the final crucifixion of Jesus, in the extermination of the human family with whom he is one....

We have to refuse to give incense—in our day, tax dollars—to our nuclear idol….I think the teaching of Jesus tells us to render to a nuclear-armed Caesar what that Caesar deserves—tax resistance. Some would call what I am urging "civil disobedience." I prefer to see it as obedience to God. (From *A Disarming Spirit: The Life of Archbishop Raymond Hunthausen*. Speech at Pacific Lutheran University, Tacoma, WA, June 12, 1981. In 1982, his tax resistance prompted the Internal Revenue Service to garnish his wages.)

Philip Berrigan

In an oddly perverse fashion, the bomb has driven us back to the Bible, and has retaught us the Sermon on the Mount. At the center of Christian life is the commandment: "Thou shalt not kill!" and its affirmation: "Love your enemies!" These two are restatements of justice and love, and of the nonviolence of Christ….

If enough Christians follow the gospel, they can bring any state to its knees. (From *Fighting the Lamb's War*, autobiography of Philip Berrigan)

St. Oscar Romero

I would like to appeal in a special way to the men of the Army, and in particular to the troops of the National Guard, the police, and the garrisons. Brothers, you belong to your own people. You kill your own brother peasants; and in the face of an order to kill that is given by a man, the law of God should prevail that says: "Do not kill!" No soldier is obliged to obey an order counter to the law of God. No one has to comply with an immoral law. It is time now that you recover your conscience and obey its dictates rather than the command of sin. (From March 23, 1980 homily at the Metropolitan Cathedral in San Salvador, the day before he was assassinated while celebrating the Eucharist)

Bishop Thomas Gumbleton

Rather than follow the lead of the Vatican and other states that have signed and ratified the Treaty on the Prohibition of Nuclear Weapons, the US now exacerbates a new nuclear arms race by upgrading every warhead and delivery system….I call on Catholics in the military, including chaplains, as well as all who work for the military or any branch of the armaments industry to heed Pope Francis's call to set aside the futility of war. All Catholics should refuse to kill and should refuse cooperation with US wars. Catholic taxpayers should make every effort to avoid paying for war and weapons. Rather, embrace Jesus, who calls us to love our enemies, put up the sword, and take up the cross. (From "A Call to Catholics: Let Us End Our Complicity in War," January 10, 2020)

James Douglass

Faith is believing that there is hope for our world. Despair is denying that our nuclear war systems can be stopped or changed. Faith is a commitment to the world's transformation through God to a Kingdom of justice and peace….Never before has our despair at changing institutions threatened the extinction of all life on earth. Faith is belief in a reality, and a transformation through which it is possible for us to live deeply enough to choose new life rather than nuclear death. A lived faith will stop the bomb.

We need to join in a community committed to that nonviolent life-force which is the power of the powerless. We need to test the truth by betting our lives on it in the world. If a community can experiment deeply enough in a nonviolent life-force the power of the Pentagon will crumble. (James Douglass, "Living at the End of the World," *Fellowship* magazine, January/February 1979)

INTERNATIONAL CAMPAIGN TO ABOLISH NUCLEAR WEAPONS NOBEL PEACE PRIZE AWARD SPEECH DECEMBER 22, 2017

Setsuko Thurlow:

Your Majesties,
Distinguished members of the Norwegian Nobel Committee,
My fellow campaigners, here and throughout the world,
Ladies and gentlemen,

It is a great privilege to accept this award, together with Beatrice, on behalf of all the remarkable human beings who form the ICAN movement. You each give me such tremendous hope that we can—and will—bring the era of nuclear weapons to an end.

I speak as a member of the family of *hibakusha*—those of us who, by some miraculous chance, survived the atomic bombings of Hiroshima and Nagasaki. For more than seven decades, we have worked for the total abolition of nuclear weapons.

We have stood in solidarity with those harmed by the production and testing of these horrific weapons around the world. People from places with long-forgotten names, like Mururoa, Ekker, Semipalatinsk, Maralinga, Bikini. People whose lands and seas were irradiated, whose bodies were experimented upon, whose cultures were forever disrupted.

We were not content to be victims. We refused to wait for an immediate fiery end or the slow poisoning of our world. We refused to sit idly in terror as the so-called great powers took us past nuclear dusk and brought us recklessly close to nuclear midnight. We rose up. We shared our stories of survival. We said: humanity and nuclear weapons cannot coexist.

Today, I want you to feel in this hall the presence of all those who perished in Hiroshima and Nagasaki. I want you to feel, above and around us, a great cloud of a quarter million souls. Each person had a name. Each person was loved by someone. Let us ensure that their deaths were not in vain.

I was just 13 years old when the United States dropped the first atomic bomb on my city, Hiroshima. I still vividly remember that morning. At 8:15, I saw a blinding bluish-white flash from the window. I remember having the sensation of floating in the air.

As I regained consciousness in the silence and darkness, I found myself pinned by the collapsed building. I began to hear my classmates' faint cries: "Mother, help me. God, help me."

Then, suddenly, I felt hands touching my left shoulder, and heard a man saying: "Don't give up! Keep pushing! I am trying to free you. See the light coming through that opening? Crawl towards it as quickly as you can." As I crawled out, the ruins were on fire. Most of my classmates in that building were burned to death alive. I saw all around me utter, unimaginable devastation.

Processions of ghostly figures shuffled by. Grotesquely wounded people, they were bleeding, burnt, blackened, and swollen. Parts of their bodies were missing. Flesh and skin hung from their bones. Some with their eyeballs hanging in their hands. Some with their bellies burst open, their intestines hanging out. The foul stench of burnt human flesh filled the air.

Thus, with one bomb my beloved city was obliterated. Most of its residents were civilians who were incinerated, vaporized, carbonized—among them, members of my own family and 351 of my schoolmates.

In the weeks, months, and years that followed, many thousands more would die, often in random and mysterious ways, from the delayed effects of radiation. Still to this day, radiation is killing survivors.

Whenever I remember Hiroshima, the first image that comes to mind is of my four-year-old nephew, Eiji—his little body transformed into an unrecognizable melted chunk of flesh. He kept begging for water in a faint voice until his death released him from agony.

To me, he came to represent all the innocent children of the world, threatened as they are at this very moment by nuclear weapons. Every second of every day, nuclear weapons endanger everyone we love and everything we hold dear. We must not tolerate this insanity any longer.

Through our agony and the sheer struggle to survive—and to rebuild our lives from the ashes—we *hibakusha* became convinced that we must warn the world about these apocalyptic weapons. Time and again, we shared our testimonies.

But still some refused to see Hiroshima and Nagasaki as atrocities—as war crimes. They accepted the propaganda that these were "good bombs" that had ended a "just war." It was this myth that led to the disastrous nuclear arms race—a race that continues to this day.

Nine nations still threaten to incinerate entire cities, to destroy life on earth, to make our beautiful world uninhabitable for future generations. The development of nuclear weapons signifies not a country's elevation to greatness, but its descent to the darkest depths of depravity. These weapons are not a necessary evil; they are the ultimate evil.

On the seventh of July this year, I was overwhelmed with joy when a great majority of the world's nations voted to adopt the Treaty on the Prohibition of Nuclear Weapons. Having witnessed humanity at its worst, I witnessed, that day, humanity at its best. We *hibakusha* had been waiting for the ban for seventy-two years. Let this be the beginning of the end of nuclear weapons.

All responsible leaders will sign this treaty. And history will judge harshly those who reject it. No longer shall their abstract theories mask the genocidal reality of their practices. No longer shall "deterrence" be viewed as anything but a deterrent to disarmament. No longer shall we live under a mushroom cloud of fear.

To the officials of nuclear-armed nations—and to their accomplices under the so-called "nuclear umbrella"—I say this: Listen to our testimony. Heed our warning. And know that your actions are consequential. You are each an integral part of a system of violence that is endangering humankind. Let us all be alert to the banality of evil.

To every president and prime minister of every nation of the world, I beseech you: Join this treaty; forever eradicate the threat of nuclear annihilation.

When I was a 13-year-old girl, trapped in the smoldering rubble, I kept pushing. I kept moving toward the light. And I survived. Our light now is the ban treaty. To all in this hall and all listening around the world, I repeat those words that I heard called to me in the ruins of Hiroshima: "Don't give up! Keep pushing! See the light? Crawl towards it."

Tonight, as we march through the streets of Oslo with torches aflame, let us follow each other out of the dark night of nuclear terror. No matter what obstacles we face, we will keep moving and keep pushing and keep sharing this light with others. This is our passion and commitment for our one precious world to survive.

(Setsuko Thurlow is a survivor of the US atomic bombing of Hiroshima. She is a leading figure in the International Campaign to Abolish Nuclear Weapons [ICAN], which won the Nobel Peace Prize in 2017. She and Beatrice Fihn, executive director of ICAN, delivered the Nobel Peace Prize lecture. Source: https://www.nobelprize.org/prizes/peace/2017/ican/lecture)

Human, economic, and environmental costs of nuclear weapons

NUCLEAR FAMINE: TWO BILLION PEOPLE AT RISK

Over the last several years, a number of studies have shown that a limited, regional nuclear war between India and Pakistan would cause significant climate disruption worldwide. In the US, corn production would decline by an average of 10 percent for an entire decade, with the most severe decline, about 20 percent, in year 5. There would be a similar decline in soybean production, with the most severe loss, again about 20 percent, in year 5. Another study found a significant decline in Chinese middle season rice production.

The decline in available food would be exacerbated by increases in food prices, which would make food inaccessible to hundreds of millions of the world's poorest. Even if agricultural markets continued to function normally, which is unlikely, 215 million people would be added to the rolls of the malnourished over the course of a decade. Turmoil in the agricultural markets would further reduce accessible food.

The 870 million people in the world who are chronically malnourished today have a baseline consumption of 1,750 calories or less per day. Even a 10 percent decline in their food consumption would put this entire group at risk.

In addition, the anticipated suspension of exports from grain-growing countries would threaten the food supplies of several hundred million additional people who have adequate nutrition today but live in countries that are highly dependent on food imports.

Finally, more than a billion people in China would face severe food insecurity. The number of people threatened by nuclear-war-induced famine would be well over two billion.

These studies demonstrate the need to move urgently to achieve a global agreement to outlaw and eliminate nuclear weapons.

Excerpted from *Executive Summary, Nuclear Famine: Two Billion People at Risk*, Ira Helfand, MD, 2013

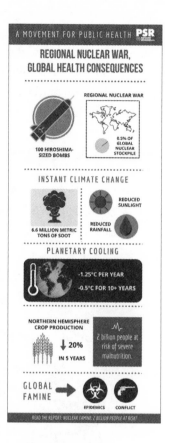

A NUCLEAR OZONE HOLE: THE GLOBAL CANCER BURDEN OF A REGIONAL NUCLEAR WAR

A nuclear war using only a small fraction of existing global arsenals would cause prolonged and catastrophic stratospheric ozone depletion. The impact on human and animal health and on fundamental ecosystems would be disastrous.

Scientists have known for more than two decades that a global nuclear war—an event that came perilously close during the Cold War between the US and the former Soviet Union and that cannot be ruled out as long as those massive arsenals exist—would severely damage the Earth's protective ozone layer. Studies in the 1980s showed that solar heating of the smoke produced by massive fires would displace and destroy significant amounts of stratospheric ozone.

Early in 2008, physicists and atmospheric scientists from the University of Colorado, UCLA, and the National Center for Atmospheric Research published important new findings that a regional nuclear conflict between India and Pakistan in which each used 50 Hiroshima-sized weapons (~15 kt) would produce an estimated 6.6 teragrams (Tg) of black carbon. In addition to the global surface cooling, large losses in stratospheric ozone would persist for years. The global mean ozone column would be depleted by as much as 25 percent for five years after the nuclear exchange. At mid-latitudes (25-45%) and at northern high latitudes (50-70%), ozone depletion would be even more severe and would last just as long.

Substantial increases in ultraviolet radiation would have serious conse-

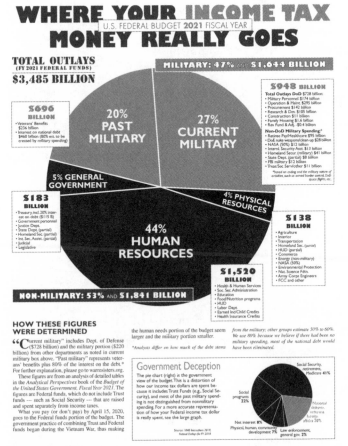

quences for human health. Those consequences, as we know from earlier studies of stratospheric ozone loss that prompted the Montreal Protocol and the phasing out of ozone depleting chlorofluorocarbons (CFCs), include steep increases in skin cancer, crop damage, and destruction of marine phytoplankton.

From *Zero Is the Only Option: Four Medical and Environmental Cases for Eradicating Nuclear Weapons*, International Physicians for the Prevention of Nuclear War.

COSTS OF WAR
Domestic, not military spending, fuels job growth

Difference in job creation
$230 BILLION ANNUAL FOR WAR VERSUS ALTERNATIVES

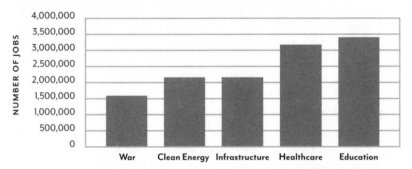

The Costs of War Project at Brown University finds that federal spending on domestic programs creates far more American jobs and yields more broad-based benefits than military spending. The study by economist Heidi Garrett-Peltier documented how many jobs are created in a variety of domestic sectors for every million dollars of federal money spent. She compared that to the number of jobs created for every $1 million spent on defense and found that domestic spending outpaces military spending in job creation by 21 percent (for wind energy development) to 178 percent (for elementary and secondary education).

"The US has a bloated military budget, and one of the reasons it has historically remained outsized is that defense spending creates jobs, both in the military and in the industries that supply goods and services to the armed forces," said Garrett-Peltier. "But when we compare federal spending on defense to the alternatives, such as health care, education, clean energy, or infrastructure, we find that all of these areas create more jobs than an equivalent amount of military spending."

Strikingly, Garrett-Peltier found that investments in elementary and secondary education create nearly three times as many American jobs as defense spending, while health care creates about twice as many jobs. Whereas $1 million spent on defense creates 6.9 direct and indirect jobs, the same amount spent on elementary and secondary education creates 19.2 jobs. One million dollars spent on healthcare creates 14.3 jobs.

Jobs per $1 million in alternative spending areas

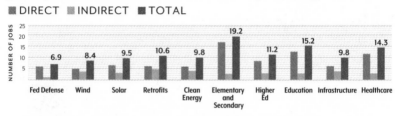

■ DIRECT   ■ INDIRECT   ■ TOTAL

$1 million in military spending creates fewer jobs than the same spending in nine other areas.

Spending on elementary and secondary education creates the most jobs, at 19.2 per $1 million.

She used an economic model to analyze how many jobs are created for every $1 million in spending, drawing on information from the US Economic Census, Internal Revenue Service tax documents, the US Bureau of Labor Statistics, US Bureau of Economic Analysis data, and other sources.

"By using the model, we can estimate both the direct and indirect jobs associated with any type of spending," Garrett-Peltier continued. That helps explain why domestic spending creates more American jobs, she noted. Some of the jobs created by defense spending "leak" overseas, whereas construction or nursing jobs created by investing in infrastructure or health care are created, and remain, in the United States.

The labor intensity involved in domestic spending is also greater than defense spending. The military is more dependent on equipment, and funds allocated might go to products, but education requires people, like teachers, aides, principals, and others.

Difference in job creation

$230 billion annual spending in defense (dark) versus alternatives (dark plus light)

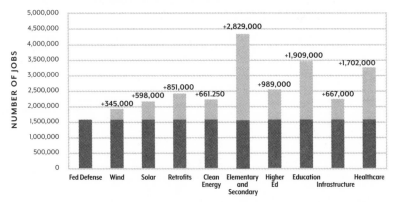

The data shows that a Trump Administration proposal to increase military spending by $54 billion would create fewer jobs than equivalent spending on health care, education, clean energy, or infrastructure and would offer less economic benefit to the nation.

"This report is especially important in helping put fact and public interest rather than myth or self-interest at the center of discussions of the Trump administration's plan for vastly increased military spending," said Catherine Lutz, co-director of the Costs of War Project.

"How our tax dollars are spent should reflect our priorities," Garrett-Peltier said. "We can have a healthier, more educated population living in a cleaner environment at the same time that we can create more jobs. Looking at the $230 billion per year that the US has been spending on strictly war-related purposes since 2001, we could have created up to 3 million more jobs if we had spent these funds on various domestic priorities rather than war."

(Source: The Costs of War Project, Brown University https://watson.brown.edu/costsofwar/)

"The DOD is the world's largest institutional user of petroleum and correspondingly, the single largest producer of greenhouse gases (GHG) in the world."

(From Pentagon Fuel Use, Climate Change and the Costs of War, June 12, 2019. Source: The Costs of War Project [see above link].)

Worldwide military expenditures were $1.8 trillion in 2018. US military spending accounted for 36 percent of total global military expenditures, nearly equal to the following eight biggest-spending countries combined.

(Source: Stockholm International Peace Research Institute Yearbook 2019. See: www.sipri.org.)

Responding as Church to nuclear weapons and gospel nonviolence

NUCLEAR DISARMAMENT IS POSSIBLE IF WE HAVE FAITH AND ACT ON IT ╬ *Arthur Laffin*

On November 10, 2017, at a special Vatican conference on "Prospects for a World Free of Nuclear Weapons and for Integral Disarmament," Pope Francis issued the most forceful condemnation of nuclear weapons of any pope to date. While previous popes have called for the elimination of nuclear weapons, Francis condemned even the "possession" of nuclear weapons (see pages 90–91), something no pope has ever done.

Francis' declaration is a major departure from the Church's prior acceptance of nuclear deterrence, which was judged as "morally acceptable" as "a step on the way toward a progressive disarmament." Francis' courageous and prophetic call marked a new moment for our Church and our world.

The Vatican conference was the first major international gathering on disarmament since 122 countries, including the Vatican, signed a new UN treaty on July 7, 2017, that calls for the complete prohibition of nuclear weapons. Conference participants included the UN high representative for disarmament affairs, NATO's deputy secretary general, eleven Nobel Peace Prize laureates, and diplomats from the US, Russia, South Korea, and Iran.

To date, neither the US and its NATO allies nor any of the other nuclear powers have endorsed the treaty.

Francis' condemnation of nuclear weapons and rejection of nuclear deterrence did not happen in a vacuum. Seventy-two years ago, at the dawn of the nuclear age, another powerful declaration was made. Immediately after the US nuclear bombings of Hiroshima and Nagasaki in August 1945, Catholic Worker co-founder Dorothy Day, the renowned disciple of gospel nonviolence and social justice, was practically a solitary religious voice in publicly condemning this unprecedented atrocity.

Day prayed and persistently labored for the abolition of nuclear weapons and war and courageously proclaimed the nonviolent mandate of Jesus. Other Catholic and Christian peacemakers in the US would follow her lead and be compelled by their faith to do the same, some of whom are now among the holy cloud of witnesses. These include Eileen Egan, Thomas Merton, OCSO, Fr. Daniel Berrigan, SJ, Philip Berrigan, Tom Lewis, Fr. Richard McSorley, SJ, Gordon Zahn, Sr. Anne Montgomery, RSCJ, Mary Jane Helrich, John Leary, Sr. Jackie Hudson, OP, Sr. Rosalie Bertell, GNSH, Judith Beaumont, Sr. Mary Evelyn Jegen, SND, Fr. George Zabelka, Larry Cloud Morgan, Sr. Chris Mulready, CSJ, Elmer Maas, Joe and Jean Gump, Ladon Sheats, Fr. Paul Kabat, OMI, Peter DeMott, Mickey Allen, Paul Mayer, Fr. Bill Bichsel, SJ, John and Teresa Grady, Anne Tucker, Fr. Jerry Zawada, OMF, Agnes and Charlie Bauerlein, Fr. Larry Rosebaugh, OMI, Bishop Walter Sullivan, Archbishop Raymond Hunthausen, Sr. Mary Luke Tobin, SL, Ed Guinan, and Bishop Leroy Matthiesen, to name but a few. Their non-violent witness, along with other peacemakers, helped pave the way for this recent papal proclamation and the Catholic Nonviolence Initiative resulting from the Just Peace Conference held at the Vatican in April 2016, which calls for the replacement of the just war theory with a theology of "just peace."

Day's commitment to nuclear abolition was unwavering. Along with Ammon Hennacy and other peace activists, she was arrested numerous times in the 1950s for protesting compulsory civil defense drills that were conducted to prepare the public for a possible nuclear attack. Day believed it was better to risk arrest and jail calling for the abolition of nuclear weapons rather than to cooperate with legally sanctioned nuclear war preparations.

In 1965, she joined twenty women and several men from different countries in a ten-day water fast in Rome, during the Second Vatican Council, to pray that the Church would issue a clear condemnation of the means of modern war. The fast was organized by the Catholic peacemaker Lanza del Vasto and his wife, Chanterelle, co-founders of the Community of the Ark in France.

At the present moment, our world stands at the nuclear brink, as evidenced by heightened tensions between the US, Iran, Russia, China, and N. Korea and upgrades being made by the US and Russia to their nuclear arsenals.

Furthermore, current US policy holds that the present US president, or any future president, could unilaterally order a nuclear attack at any time.

The Bulletin of the Atomic Scientists "Doomsday Clock" is now at 100 seconds before midnight due to the dangers of nuclear war and the climate crisis.

With the very future of human survival and our planet's existence at stake, Francis' new exhortation for disarmament offers a concrete way to avert global catastrophe. But how can we make this call for disarmament real for our time?

First and foremost, we must have the faith, courage, and will to believe that total nuclear disarmament can occur.

If we are to take seriously the magnitude of the nuclear threat and the admonition of Francis, we must risk taking action that is commensurate with the colossal threat we face. Therefore, if it is wrong to possess nuclear weapons, then it is equally wrong to build and modernize them. And if it is wrong to build and modernize them, then no Catholic or follower of Jesus can participate in the chain of command to ever use them.

Consequently, if there is unanimous consent to refuse to build, upgrade, and use these weapons of mass destruction, then they can be permanently dismantled.

Living in a nation that has legally sanctioned nuclear weapons and relies on them for its ultimate security, what would Jesus have us do? Clearly, Jesus teaches that you cannot serve both God and mammon and that we must place our trust in God for our true security. He calls us to disarm our hearts of fear, hate, and greed. He instructs us to forever put away the sword. He calls us to love our enemies and never to kill.

Since the beginning of the Manhattan Project in 1942 to 1996, about $5.8 trillion ($9.3 trillion in present-day terms) was spent on the US nuclear weapons program. And since 1998, it is estimated that over $300 billion has been spent on the US nuclear arsenal. A thirty-year $1.7 trillion modernization of the US nuclear arsenal is now underway.

With respect to producing and upgrading nuclear weapons and being involved with their use today, can followers of Jesus be employed in such weapons-related work? Christians who work in such jobs are faced with a serious faith and moral dilemma. The following insights from Catholic peacemakers serve to counsel us on this matter.

Fr. McSorley stated in *New Testament Basis of Peacemaking*:

> We cannot seriously imagine Jesus pushing the button to launch a nuclear bomb, or registering for the draft, or wearing the uniform of any national state, or paying taxes for nuclear weapons, or working in a plant that manufactures weapons of death.

And Pope Paul VI, in a speech to the diplomatic corps on February 10, 1972, made this pronouncement:

> The conversion of military manufacturing plants and military markets for civilian purposes is equally possible, if trouble is taken to plan ahead. It is all the more feasible in that it would create jobs by making it possible to undertake the large-scale projects which prove necessary for the protection of the environment and the satisfaction of human needs.
>
> Refusal to undertake this conversion is completely incompatible with the spirit of humanity and still more with the spirit of Christianity because "it is unthinkable that no other work can be found for hundreds of thousands of workers than the production of instruments of death."

Dorothy Day made a similar appeal (see page 93).

We also need to consider the example of the late Bishop Leroy Matthiesen, who told the Catholics in his diocese who worked at the

Pantex nuclear weapons plant in Amarillo, Texas: "In the name of the God of peace, quit your jobs." In making this appeal, he said he would try to offer financial assistance to any defense worker who would quit.

There is also the witness of former defense worker Bob Aldridge (see page 52).

The most significant voices that we need to hear and learn from in the struggle to abolish nuclear weapons are those of the atomic bomb survivors, known as *hibakusha*, one of whom, representing an organization from Japan made up exclusively of atomic bomb survivors, was present at the 2017 Vatican conference.

The *hibakusha* have been relentless in the pursuit to forever rid the world of nuclear weapons. Their presence is a constant living reminder of our need as a nation to repent for the development and use of nuclear weapons and to eliminate them.

In recognizing the vital importance of the *hibakusha*, Francis stated at the disarmament conference: "Essential … is the witness given by the *hibakusha*, the survivors of the bombing of Hiroshima and Nagasaki, together with other victims of nuclear arms testing. May their prophetic voice serve as a warning, above all for coming generations!"

During Francis' visit to Nagasaki and Hiroshima in 2019, he movingly remembered the victims of the US atomic bombings and reiterated the urgent plea of the Hibakusha to abolish all nuclear weapons.

I personally owe the *hibakusha* a deep debt of gratitude for inspiring me in my journey of peacemaking when I met them during the first United Nations Special Session on Disarmament in 1978. At that time, they called on the nuclear powers of the world to ban nuclear weapons.

Ultimately, if true disarmament is to occur, we must first repent of the nuclear sin. Such acts of repentance have already taken place. There have been delegations of US Catholic peacemakers who have gone to Japan to personally apologize and ask forgiveness for the US atomic bombings of the Japanese.

And on August 6, 2016, the anniversary date of the US bombing of Hiroshima, members of the Catholic Worker, Pax Christi, and other peace groups held a prayer service of repentance in front of the White House. During the service an "apology petition" was presented to a *hibakusha*.

Signed by more than 700 people, the petition called on the US government to join the signatories in apologizing to Japan for using the bomb against them and pledging to work for total nuclear abolition.

The nuclear challenge before us is great but not insurmountable, for with God, and people acting on their faith convictions, all things are possible. History bears out this truth. Slavery was abolished. Legal segregation ended in the United States. Apartheid ended in South Africa. The Berlin Wall came down.

Drawing on the rich biblical tradition of nonviolence and the many examples of nonviolent resistance in human history, Plowshares activists have been inspired to carry out over 100 disarmament actions since 1980, whereby the nuclear swords of our time have symbolically been beaten into plowshares (Isaiah 2:4 and Micah 4:3). The most recent plowshares action, the Kings Bay Plowshares 7, took place on April 4, 2018, the 50th anniversary of the assassination of Martin Luther King Jr., at the Naval Submarine Base Kings Bay in St. Mary's, Georgia. The base is homeport for six Trident nuclear submarines, with each submarine having the capacity to cause devastation equivalent to between 1,000 and 4,000 Hiroshima bombs. They declared in their action statement: "Nuclear weapons eviscerate the rule of law, enforce white supremacy, perpetuate endless war and environmental destruction, and ensure impunity for all manner of crimes against humanity. Dr. King said, 'The ultimate logic of racism is genocide.' We say, 'The ultimate logic of Trident is omnicide.'" In October 2019, they were tried and convicted by a jury of three felonies and a misdemeanor in US District Court in Brunswick, Georgia (see page 125 for sentencing information).

There have also been countless other vigils, fasts, and nonviolent resistance actions for disarmament and ending war. I have been blessed to be part of many such actions, including two Plowshares actions directed at the first-strike Trident nuclear submarine.

On September 4, 1989, six peacemakers and I carried out the Thames River Plowshares action in New London, Connecticut. We were able to swim and canoe to the docked USS Pennsylvania, the 10th Trident, and hammered and poured blood on the hull. Three of us, including myself, were able to climb on top of the submarine, where we prayed for the abolition of nuclear weapons.

From aboard this most destructive weapon, I believed then, and I believe now, that if people have the faith to believe that disarmament is possible, and act on that faith, it can occur. I, along with other Plowshares activists and many other peacemakers, know this can happen because we were able to begin the process of true disarmament.

The Catholic Church and all churches have a crucial role to play in implementing Francis' declaration to bring about a disarmed world.

What if the Church could take the lead in calling for the conversion of arms industries to non-military production, while advocating for full and just protection of workers' rights during the transition process? What if the Church would provide material resources for those who quit their jobs for reasons of conscience? What if the Church leadership in all denominations were to call on all Christians in the nuclear chain of command to refuse orders to use nuclear weapons, and for all Christians to publicly support those who do so? What if the pope's statement was proclaimed in every diocese, at every parish, and in every Catholic school, college, and seminary?

And what if the US bishops and all Catholics and Christians in the US demanded that the US government sign the UN Treaty on the Prohibition of Nuclear Weapons? What if Christians in other nuclear nations would make the same appeal to their governments? These efforts would go a long way to help create the climate necessary to bring about real disarmament.

Now is the time to act. Now is the time to enflesh God's dream of beating all the swords (weapons) of our time into plowshares!

(A version of this article first appeared in the *National Catholic Reporter Online edition*, December 14, 2017, and was revised in February 2020)

Vow of nonviolence

Many people have taken the Vow of Nonviolence since it was composed by Eileen Egan and Rev. John Dear and circulated by Pax Christi. It can be taken privately, with a local peace community, as part of a parish liturgy, or any other way that suits you. Many profess the vow each year as part of their New Year observance.

RECOGNIZING THE VIOLENCE IN MY OWN HEART, yet trusting in the goodness and mercy of God, I vow for one year to practice the nonviolence of Jesus who taught us in the Sermon on the Mount:

"Blessed are the peacemakers, for they shall be called the sons and daughters of God....You have learned how it was said, 'You must love your neighbor and hate your enemy'; but I say to you, Love your enemies, and pray for those who persecute you. In this way, you will be daughters and sons of your Creator in heaven."

I vow to carry out in my life the love and example of Jesus:

by striving for peace within myself and seeking to be a peacemaker in my daily life;

by refusing to retaliate in the face of provocation and violence;

by persevering in nonviolence of tongue and heart;

by living conscientiously and simply so that I do not deprive others of the means to live;

by actively resisting evil and working nonviolently to abolish war and the causes of war from my own heart and from the face of the earth.

God, I trust in your sustaining love and believe that just as you gave me the grace and desire to offer this, so you will also bestow abundant grace to fulfill it.

(For more info, contact Pax Christi USA)

CATHOLIC NONVIOLENCE INITIATIVE

The Catholic Nonviolence Initiative (https://nonviolencejustpeace.net), a project of Pax Christi International, the Catholic peace movement, affirms that active nonviolence is at the heart of the vision and message of Jesus, the life of the Catholic Church, and the long-term vocation of healing and reconciling all people to one another and to the planet.

This bold effort was launched at the Nonviolence and Just Peace Conference held in Rome April 11–13, 2016, and was co-sponsored by the Pontifical Council for Justice and Peace, Pax Christi International, and other international bodies (see full list below).

Laypeople, theologians, members of religious congregations, priests, and bishops from Africa, the Americas, Asia, Europe, the Middle East, and Oceania gathered to call on the Catholic Church to take a clear stand for active nonviolence and against all forms of violence. In his message to the conference, Pope Francis said, "Your thoughts on revitalizing the tools of nonviolence, and of active nonviolence in particular, will be a needed and positive contribution."

An appeal to the Catholic Church to recommit
to the centrality of gospel nonviolence

The following statement, crafted in a consensus process, was released at the end of the Nonviolence and Just Peace conference in Rome, April 2016. Hundreds of organizations and thousands of individuals have signed the appeal.

As Christians committed to a more just and peaceful world we are called to take a clear stand for creative and active nonviolence and against all forms of violence. With this conviction, and in recognition of the Jubilee Year of Mercy declared by Pope Francis, people from many countries gathered at the Nonviolence and Just Peace Conference sponsored by the Pontifical Council for Justice and Peace and Pax Christi International on April 11–13, 2016, in Rome.

Our assembly, people of God from Africa, the Americas, Asia, Europe, the Middle East, and Oceania, included laypeople, theologians, members of religious congregations, priests, and bishops. Many of us live in communities experiencing violence and oppression. All of us are practitioners of justice and peace. We are grateful for the message to our conference from Pope Francis: "Your thoughts on revitalizing the tools of nonviolence, and of active nonviolence in particular, will be a needed and positive contribution".

Looking at our world today

We live in a time of tremendous suffering, widespread trauma, and fear linked to militarization, economic injustice, climate change, and myriad other specific forms of violence. In this context, those of us who stand in the Christian tradition are called to recognize the centrality of active nonviolence to the vision and message of Jesus; to the life and practice of the Catholic Church; and to our long-term vocation of healing and reconciling both people and the planet.

We rejoice in the rich concrete experiences of people engaged in work for peace around the world, many of whose stories we heard during this

conference. They illuminate the creativity and power of nonviolent practices in many different situations of potential or actual violent conflict.
Recent academic research, in fact, has confirmed that nonviolent resistance
strategies are twice as effective as violent ones.

The time has come for our Church to be a living witness and to invest
far greater human and financial resources in promoting a spirituality and
practice of active nonviolence and in forming and training our Catholic
communities in effective nonviolent practices. In all of this, Jesus is our
inspiration and model.

Jesus and nonviolence

In his own times, rife with structural violence, Jesus proclaimed a new, nonviolent order rooted in the unconditional love of God. Neither passive nor
weak, Jesus' nonviolence was the power of love in action. In vision and
deed, he is the revelation and embodiment of the Nonviolent God, a truth
especially illuminated in the cross and resurrection. He calls us to develop
the virtue of nonviolent peacemaking.

Clearly, the Word of God, the witness of Jesus, should never be used to
justify violence, injustice, or war. We confess that the people of God have
betrayed this central message of the gospel many times, participating in
wars, persecution, oppression, exploitation, and discrimination.

We believe that there is no "just war." Too often the "just war theory"
has been used to endorse rather than prevent or limit war. Suggesting that
a "just war" is possible also undermines the moral imperative to develop
tools and capacities for nonviolent transformation of conflict.

We need a new framework that is consistent with gospel nonviolence. A
different path is clearly unfolding in recent Catholic social teaching. Pope
John XXIII wrote that war is not a suitable way to restore rights; Pope Paul
VI linked peace and development, and told the UN "no more war"; Pope
John Paul II said that "war belongs to the tragic past, to history"; Pope
Benedict XVI said that "loving the enemy is the nucleus of the Christian
revolution"; and Pope Francis said, "The true strength of the Christian is
the power of truth and love, which leads to the renunciation of all violence.
Faith and violence are incompatible." He has also urged the "abolition
of war."

We propose that the Catholic Church develop and consider shifting to a just peace approach based on gospel nonviolence. A just peace approach offers a vision and an ethic to build peace as well as to prevent, defuse, and to heal the damage of violent conflict. This ethic includes a commitment to human dignity and thriving relationships, with specific criteria, virtues, and practices to guide our actions. We recognize that peace requires justice, and justice requires peacemaking.

Living gospel nonviolence and just peace
In that spirit we commit ourselves to furthering Catholic understanding and practice of active nonviolence on the road to just peace. As would-be disciples of Jesus, challenged and inspired by stories of hope and courage in these days, we call on the Church we love to:

- continue developing Catholic social teaching on nonviolence. In particular, we call on Pope Francis to share with the world an encyclical on nonviolence and just peace;

- integrate gospel nonviolence explicitly into the life, including the sacramental life, and work of the Church through dioceses, parishes, agencies, schools, universities, seminaries, religious orders, voluntary associations, and others;

- promote nonviolent practices and strategies (e.g., nonviolent resistance, restorative justice, trauma healing, unarmed civilian protection, conflict transformation, and peacebuilding strategies);

- initiate a global conversation on nonviolence within the Church, with people of other faiths, and with the larger world to respond to the monumental crises of our time with the vision and strategies of nonviolence and just peace;

- no longer use or teach "just war theory"; continue advocating for the abolition of war and nuclear weapons;

- lift up the prophetic voice of the church to challenge unjust world powers and to support and defend those nonviolent activists whose work for peace and justice put their lives at risk.

In every age, the Holy Spirit graces the Church with the wisdom to respond to the challenges of its time. In response to what is a global epidemic of violence, which Pope Francis has labeled a "world war in installments," we are being called to invoke, pray over, teach, and take decisive action. With our communities and organizations, we look forward to continue collaborating with the Holy See and the global Church to advance gospel nonviolence.

(Conference sponsors. In addition to the Pontifical Council for Justice and Peace and Pax Christi International, the Nonviolence and Just Peace conference was sponsored by the Justice and Peace Commission of the Union of International Superiors General/Union of Superiors General, the Conference of Major Superiors of Men, the Leadership Conference of Women Religious, Maryknoll missioners, St. Columban's Mission Society, and Pace e Bene Nonviolence Service.)

TAKING ACTION FOR DISARMAMENT

Acting as faith communities in response to the moral and spiritual problems of our day is what being Church is all about. These personal, intentional Christian communities constitute the vibrant and hopeful church of our day, a phenomenon often unseen by those who view church merely as institution. The responsibility of our faith belongs to such communities as these, as it once did to the community around Jesus: to live and proclaim the gospel.

God's commandment "Thou shalt not kill" must be upheld by all followers of Jesus. Any government that legally sanctions violence and killing of any form violates God's command and must be nonviolently resisted. As Church in a nuclear society, our communities bear the particular responsibility to challenge and reverse the continued reliance on nuclear weapons and the values that support it in the name of the gospel. The task is extraordinarily immense. However, it is the faith aspect of our communities that enables us to let God measure the worth of our action rather than to measure it ourselves. Prayer is the ultimate expression of this faith; it keeps us both hopeful and modest. Action based in open prayer and a common faith offers a greater promise and endurance than normal expectation would allow. This dynamic relation of prayer and action is integral to the response that true discipleship demands of us.

A large part of our peace and justice ministry as Church consists in educating and raising consciousness about gospel nonviolence and nuclear weapons. The conflict of Kingdom and worldly values in our culture is immediately evident in the way in which the question of nuclear weapons is generally considered in government and in the mass media. The human life issue, it seems, is almost always lost in the debate about international and domestic economic and political matters. The values of human life are absolutely primary for the Christian disciple. Our efforts at educating ourselves and others should reflect this priority of values.

Examples of this education include developing prayer and study groups that focus on the problem of nuclear weapons; distributing literature at churches, schools, and work sites; doing outreach to media; encouraging local clergy to acquaint their congregations with particular church statements about nuclear weapons; petitioning city councils and state and congressional representatives to take the ICAN Parliamentary Pledge and pass resolutions/legislation adopting the UN Treaty on the Prohibition of Nuclear Weapons (see ICAN, page 123); and relating to other communities and churches in your region engaged in peace and social justice work.

Undertaking research on local war industry contracts helps to illustrate the extent to which the production, deployment, and maintenance of nuclear weapons concretely affects our own cities and towns as well as the jobs they offer. Good sources of data for this are the Don't Bank On The Bomb and Nuclear Ban US websites (listed in the resources section), which provide information on financial institutions that fund nuclear weapons production and on the companies that make nuclear weapons.

Social action for justice and peace is a constitutive element of the gospel mandate. The link between the concerns of justice and peace are found in the economic basis of war itself as well as in the effects of war in our society and in the world—namely, poverty. As followers of Jesus who identify with the poor and the oppressed, we are obliged to deal with the poverty around us: to serve its victims and to work toward the elimination of its causes. Addressing the problems of human need locally by responding to them in personal service also helps expose in human terms the priority given to war-making systems rather than to life-supporting systems in our culture. (See groups: Catholic Worker and Poor People's Campaign.)

Coupled with these healing forms of action is the radical witness of nonviolent resistance actions. God's law supersedes human law. Followers of Jesus, acting in obedience to God's command to love and never to kill, have a moral right and duty to resist laws that sanction injustice, death, and destruction. Acts of nonviolent resistance follow in the tradition of Jesus' cleansing of the temple and in the nonviolent movements and actions, from biblical times until now, that have helped bring about social transformation (i.e., abolition movement, women's suffrage movement, civil rights movement, and anti-Vietnam War movement). Examples of actions include developing a disarmament-peace conversion campaign organized around a local nuclear weapons research or production plant; organizing public vigils at local Congressional offices or at a nuclear weapons plant; engaging in nonviolent civil resistance (divine obedience) at such locations; resisting the payment of the portion of one's federal taxes used to finance the military budget; and leaving a military research or production job for reasons of faith and conscience. A faith community or congregation might also consider providing housing and financial support to a worker who has left war-related employment for reasons of conscience.

There are many, many more ideas for church action for peace. An openness to the working of the Spirit will inform your action choices as well as the actions themselves. The national and local groups and resources listed in this appendix will hopefully be helpful in providing you with more information and ideas. Please make sure to check the websites for Groups Doing Grassroots Disarmament Work and all other group listings, as you may be able to get involved with one of these groups. Developing a peace and justice ministry is a fragile and vulnerable struggle, yet out of this experience emerges new life and hope.

Groups working on national and local levels for disarmament, social justice, and advocating nonviolence

Catholic Worker
catholicworker.org *(information about Catholic Worker and listing of communities)*

Fellowship of Reconciliation
forusa.org *(provides listing of different denominational peace fellowships)*

Center on Conscience and War
centeronconscience.org

Veterans for Peace
veteransforpeace.org

Franciscan Action Network (WDC)
franciscanaction.org

Jonah House (Baltimore)
jonahhouse.org

CODEPINK
codepink.org

National War Tax Resistance Coordinating Committee
https://nwtrcc.org

Nonviolence International (WDC)
nonviolenceinternational.net

Pace e Bene Nonviolence Service/Campaign Nonviolence
paceebene.org; campaignnonviolence.org

Bartimaeus Cooperative Ministries
bcm-net.org

Maryknoll Office for Global Concerns
maryknollogc.org

Pacific Life Community
pacificlifecommunity.wordpress.com

Pax Christi USA (WDC)
paxchristiusa.org

Pax Christi International
paxchristi.net

Poor People's Campaign
Poorpeoplescampaign.org

Witness Against Torture
witnessagainsttorture.com

Sojourners (WDC)
Sojo.net

Red Letter Christians (Philadelphia)
redletterchristians.org

US Conference of Catholic Bishops
Office of International Justice and Peace: usccb.org

Voices for Creative Nonviolence (Chicago)
vcnv.org

Center for Christian Nonviolence
centerforchristiannonviolence.org

Friends of Franz Jagerstatter and Ben Salmon
https://www.bensalmon.org/about-friends-of-franz-and-ben.html

Christian Peacemaker Teams
CPT.org

Little Friends for Peace
lffp.org

Jubilee USA
Jubileeusa.org

SOA Watch
soaw.org

RESOURCES

Move the Nuclear Weapons Money (nuclearweaponsmoney.org).
International campaign to cut nuclear weapons budgets, invest
in critical human needs and divest in companies manufacturing
nuclear weapons components and delivery systems.

*All of the above contain links to other web resources
and lead to other sources of information and ideas.*

Important websites for groups doing grassroots disarmament work

Alliance for Nuclear Accountability (ananuclear.org). Network of local,
regional, and national organizations working collaboratively on issues of nuclear
weapons production and waste cleanup. Members organizations are watchdogs
of the Department of Energy's nuclear weapons and energy programs.

PeaceWorks KC (peaceworkskc.org). Nonviolent campaign for
disarmament at the Kansas City Nuclear Weapons Plant.

Tri-Valley CARES (trivalleycares.org). Nonviolent campaign for disarmament
at Lawrence Livermore National Nuclear Weapons Lab in California.

Los Alamos Peace Project (networkearth.org). Nonviolent campaign
for disarmament at Los Alamos Nuclear Labs in New Mexico.

Oak Ridge Environmental Peace Alliance—OREPA (orepa.org).
Nonviolent campaign for disarmament at the Y-12 Nuclear
Weapons Complex in Oak Ridge, Tennessee.

Ground Zero Center for Nonviolent Action (www.gzcenter.org).
Nonviolent campaign for disarmament at Naval Base Kitsap-Bangor
in Silverdale, WA, where eight Trident submarines are based.

Brandywine Peace Community (brandywinepeace.org). Nonviolent
campaign for disarmament at Lockheed Martin in the Philadelphia area.

Global Network Against Weapons and Nuclear Power in Space (space4peace.
org). Organizes International Campaign to stop the militarization of space
and ending the use of nuclear technology in space. Focuses on: No Space
Force; No Missile Defense; Close US/NATO Bases Worldwide (there are
an estimated 800 bases worldwide); End Privatization of Foreign/Military
Policy; Convert the Military Industrial Complex; Address Climate Change
and Global Poverty. Contact for nonviolent resistance and economic
conversion campaign at General Dynamics/Bath Iron Works in Bath, Maine.

Kings Bay Plowshares 7 (kingsbayplowshares7.org). Seven Catholics who carried out a Plowshares action directed at the Trident submarine program at the Naval Submarine Base Kings Bay in St. Mary's, Georgia, on April 4, 2018. They were tried, convicted, and, as of this writing, Liz McAlister will be sentenced by video conferencing on June 8, 2020; the other six requested to appear in court for sentencing and are awaiting confirmation of a date. See KBP7 support group web site for more information. Also see Beyond Trident Campaign-Nuclear Watch South (nonukesyall.org).

The Nuclear Resister (nukeresister.org). Documents nonviolent resistance actions in the US and worldwide for a peaceful and nuclear-free future. Includes updated list of imprisoned anti-nuclear and war resisters.

Nukewatch (nukewatchinfo.org). Grassroots nuclear watchdog that brings critical attention to the locations, movements, dangers, and politics of nuclear weapons and radioactive waste.

Nevada Desert Experience (nevadadesertexperience.org). Nonviolent campaign for nuclear disarmament at the Nevada National Security Site, previously known as Nevada Test Site.

Los Angeles Catholic Worker (lacatholicworker.org). Contact for nonviolent resistance campaign for nuclear disarmament at Vandenberg Air Force Base in California.

Des Moines Catholic Worker (dmcatholicworker.org). Contact for nonviolent resistance campaign for disarmament at Offutt Air Force Base, home of US Strategic Command (STRATCOM).

Norfolk Catholic Worker (www.catholicworker.org/communities/houses/va-norfolk-norfolk-catholic-worker.html). Contact for nonviolent civil resistance witness for disarmament at Norfolk Naval Base and Newport News Shipbuilding.

Dorothy Day Catholic Worker (dccatholicworker.wordpress.com). Contact for nonviolent witness and civil resistance actions for abolishing war, nuclear weapons, and all weapons; total demilitarization; and social justice at the Pentagon and White House.

For information about nonviolent witness and civil resistance actions to end US killer-drone attacks see CODEPINK and The Nuclear Resister (already listed), and upstatedroneaction.org, shutdowncreech.blogspot.com, knowdrones.com, and paxchristimdcb.org.

BOOKS

Robert J. Aldridge, *First Strike*. South End Press, 1999.

Genevieve "Mickey" Allen, *Chip on My Shoulder*. Instant Publisher.Com, 2003.

William J. Barber II and Jonathan Wilson-Hartgrove,
*The Third Reconstruction: How a Moral Movement Is Overcoming
the Politics of Division and Fear*. Beacon Press, 2016.

Daniel Berrigan, *Testimony: The Word Made Fresh*. Orbis Books, 2005.

Daniel Berrigan, *To Dwell in Peace*. HarperCollins, 1988.

Frida Berrigan, *It Runs in the Family*. OR Books, 2014.

Philip Berrigan, *Fighting the Lamb's War: Skirmishes
with the American Empire*. iUniverse, 2011.

Philip Berrigan and Elizabeth McAlister,
The Time's Discipline. Wipf and Stock, 2011.

Wes Howard Brook, *Come Out My People: God's Call
out of Empire and Beyond*. Orbis Books, 2010.

Wes Howard Brook, *Empire Baptized: How the Church Embraced
What Jesus Rejected (Second–Fifth Centuries)*. Orbis Books, 2016.

Ken Butigan, *Nonviolent Lives: People and Movements Changing the
World Through the Power of Active Nonviolence*. Pace e Bene, 2016.

Shane Claiborne, *The Irresistible Revolution:
Living as an Ordinary Radical*. Zondervan, 2006.

Ramsey Clark, *The Fire This Time: U.S. War Crimes
in the Gulf*. Thunder's Mouth Press, 1992.

James Cone, *The Cross and The Lynching Tree*. Orbis Books, 2013.

Frances Crowe, *Finding My Radical Soul: A Memoir*. Haley's, 2015.

Dorothy Day, *The Long Loneliness*. HarperOne, 2009.

Sam Day, *Crossing the Line*. Fortkamp Publishing Co., 1991.

John Dear, *The Beatitudes of Peace: Meditations on the Beatitudes,
Peacemaking and the Spiritual Life*. Twenty-Third Publications, 2016.

John Dear, *The Nonviolent Life*. Pace e Bene, 2013.

John Dear, *A Persistent Peace: An Autobiography*. Loyola Press, 2008.

John Dear, *They Will Inherit the Earth: Peace and Nonviolence
in a Time of Climate Change*. Orbis Books, 2018.

John Dear, *Walking the Way: Following Jesus on the Journey of Gospel Nonviolence to the Cross and Resurrection*. Twenty-Third Publications, 2015.

David Dellinger, *From Yale to Jail*. Pantheon Books, 1993.

Marie Dennis, editor, *Choosing Peace: The Catholic Church Returns to Gospel Nonviolence*. Orbis Books, 2018.

Jeff Dietrich, *The Good Samaritan: Stories from the Los Angeles Catholic Worker on Skid Row*. Tsehai Publishers, 2014.

Jeff Dietrich, *Reluctant Resister*. Unicorn Press, 1983.

James Douglass, *JFK and the Unspeakable: Why He Died and Why It Matters*. Orbis Books, 2008; Touchstone, 2010.

James Douglass, *The Nonviolent Coming of God*. Orbis Books, 1992; Wipf and Stock, 2006.

Dave Eberhardt, *For All the Saints: A Protest Primer*. Self-Published, 2017.

Paul Elie, *The Life You Save May Be Your Own: An American Pilgrimage*. Farrar, Straus and Giroux, 2003.

Robert Ellsberg, *All Saints: Daily Reflections on Saints, Prophets, and Witnesses for Our Time*. Crossroad Publishing Company, 1997.

Robert Ellsberg, editor, *Dorothy Day: Selected Writings*. Orbis Books, 2005.

James Forest, *Loving Our Enemies: Reflections on the Hardest Commandment*. Orbis Books, 2014.

Frank Fromherz, *A Disarming Spirit: The Life of Archbishop Raymond Hunthausen*. Tsehai Publishing, 2019.

Bruce Gagnon, *Come Together Right Now: Organizing Stories from a Fading Empire*. Just Write Books, 2005.

M.K. Gandhi, *Non-Violent Resistance*. Schocken Books, 1967; Dover Publications, 2001.

Ann Fagan Ginger, editor, *Nuclear Weapons Are Illegal: The Historic Opinion of the World Court and How It Will Be Enforced*. The Apex Press, 1998.

David Hartsough, *Waging Peace: Global Adventures of a Lifelong Activist*. PM Press, 2014.

Vincent Intondi, *African Americans against the Bomb: Nuclear Weapons, Colonialism, and the Black Freedom Movement*. Stanford University Press, 2015.

Bill Wylie-Kellermann, editor, *A Keeper of the Word: Selected Writings by William Stringfellow*. Eerdmans Publishing Company, 1994.

Bill Wylie-Kellermann, *Seasons of Faith and Conscience*. Orbis Books, 1991.

Judith Kelly, *Just Call Me Jerzy: Popieluszko in the United States and Canada*. FxBEAR Publishing, 2016.

Martin Luther King Jr., *Strength to Love*. Fortress, 1982, 2010.

Arthur Laffin and Anne Montgomery, co-editors, *Swords into Plowshares: Nonviolent Direct Action for Disarmament*. Harper & Row, 1987.

Arthur Laffin and Anne Montgomery, co-editors, *Swords into Plowshares (Volume One)*. 1996. Wipf and Stock Publishers, 2010.

Arthur Laffin, *Swords Into Plowshares (Volume Two): A Chronology of Plowshares-Disarmament Actions 1980–2003*. Wipf and Stock, 2010.

Robert J. Lifton, *The Climate Swerve: Reflections on Mind, Hope and Survival*. The New Press, 2017.

Robert J. Lifton and Richard Falk, *Indefensible Weapons: The Political and Psychological Case Against Nuclearism*. Basic Books, 1982, House of Anansi Pr, 1998.

Charles J. Liteky, *Renunciation: My Pilgrimage from Catholic Military Chaplain, Vietnam Hawk, and Medal of Honor Recipient to Civilian Warrior for Peace*. Charles J. Liteky and Judith Liteky Balch Liteky Trust, 2017.

Eduard Loring, *The Cry of the Poor: Cracking White Male Supremacy*. Open Door Community Press, 2010.

Catherine Maresca, *Violence and Nonviolence in Scripture: Helping Children Understand Challenging Stories*. Liturgy Training Publications, 2019.

Eric Martin and Daniel Cosacchi, *The Berrigan Letters*. Orbis Books, 2016.

Colman McCarthy, *I'd Rather Teach Peace*. Orbis Books, 2003, 2008.

Eli S. McCarthy, *A Just Peace Ethic Primer*. Georgetown University Press, 2020.

Richard McSorley, SJ, *New Testament Basis of Peacemaking*. Herald Press, 1985.

Richard McSorley, SJ (John Dear, editor), *It's a Sin to Build a Nuclear Weapon*. Fortkamp Publishing Co. 1991; Wipf and Stock, 2010.

Thomas Merton, *Peace in the Post-Christian Era*. Orbis Books, 2004.

Ched Myers, *Binding the Strong Man: A Political Reading of Mark's Story of Jesus*. Orbis Books, 1988.

Ched Myers, *Who Will Roll Away the Stone?* Orbis Books, 1994.

Liane Ellison Norman, *Hammer of Justice: Molly Rush and the Plowshares Eight*. Pittsburgh Peace Institute Books, 1989.

Henri Nouwen, *The Road to Peace: Writings on Peace and Justice*. Edited by John Dear. Orbis Books, 2002.

Pope Francis, *Laudato Si: On Care for Our Common Home*. Our Sunday Visitor, 2015.

Prince of Peace Plowshares, *Disciples and Dissidents: Prison Writings of the Prince of Peace Plowshares*. Haley's, 2001.

Rosalie Riegel, *Doing Time for Peace: Resistance, Family and Community*. Vanderbilt University Press, 2013.

Rosalie Riegel, *Crossing the Line: Nonviolent Resisters Speak Out for Peace*. Cascade Books, 2013.

Jeremy Scahill, *Dirty Wars: The World Is a Battlefield*. Nation Books, 2013.

Scott Schaeffer-Duffy, *Nothing Is Impossible: Stories from the Life of a Catholic Worker*. Haley's, 2016.

Suzanne Belote Shanley and Brayton Shanley, *Loving Life on the Margins: The Story of the Agape Community*. Haley's, 2019.

Bryan Stevenson, *Just Mercy*. Spiegel & Grau, 2015.

William Stringfellow, *An Ethic for Christians and Other Aliens in a Strange Land*. Word, 1973; Wipf and Stock, 2004.

Louie Vitale, OFM, *Love Is What Matters: Writings on Peace and Nonviolence*. Edited by Ken Butigan. Pace e Bene, 2015.

Jim Wallis, *Christ in Crisis: Why We Need to Reclaim Jesus*. HarperOne, 2019.

Brendan Walsh and Willa Bickham, *The Long Loneliness in Baltimore*. Apprentice House, 2016.

James Melvin Washington, *A Testament of Hope: Essential Writings of Martin Luther King, Jr.* Harper & Row, 1986; HarperOne, 2003.

Cornell West, *Black Prophetic Fire*. Beacon Press, 2014.

S. Brian Willson, *On Third World Legs*. Charles H. Kerr, 1992.

Walter Wink, *Engaging the Powers: Discernment and Resistance in a World of Domination*. Fortress Press, 1992.

Witness Against Torture, *Witness Against Torture: The Campaign to Shut Down Guantanamo*. Yellow Bike Press, 2008.

Scott Wright, *Oscar Romero and the Communion of the Saints*. Orbis Books, 2016.

Gordon Zahn, *In Solitary Witness: The Life and Death of Franz Jagerstatter*. Beacon Press, 1964. Revised edition; Templegate Publishers, 1986.

Angie Zelter, *Trident on Trial*. Luath Press Limited, 2001.

Howard Zinn, *The People's History of the United States*. Harper Perrenial, 2015.

MULTIMEDIA

Command and Control: The Day Our Luck Almost Ran Out (210 minutes), a documentary about the Damascus Incident, the core of Eric Schlosser's book *Command and Control* (see book list).

The Forgotten Bomb (95 minutes), a film exploring our tendency to ignore the presence of nuclear weapons. Produced by Bud Ryan and Stuart Overbey. https://www.forgottenbomb.com/.

The Nuns, The Priests and the Bombs (105 minutes), a film about nonviolent direct actions to disarm the nuclear weapons establishment in the US. Produced by Helen Young. https://nunspriestsbombsthefilm.com/.

"A Time Lapse Map of Every Nuclear Explosion Since 1945," https://www.youtube.com/watch?v=LLCF7vPanrY.

"How Close Do You Live to a Nuclear Bomb?" https://www.youtube.com/watch?v=HZXn5Ct0PJg.

Thirty Seconds to Midnight (92 minutes). Humanity is on the brink of extinction! America's reckless provocations of both Russia and China, two nuclear-armed countries, risk a nuclear holocaust from which no one survives. Climate change and global warming, if not mitigated immediately, will end the human experiment on earth. Produced by Regis Tremblay. http://registremblay.com/product/thirty-seconds-midnight/.

Joining the Conversation (4 minutes, 10 seconds), https://www.youtube.com/watch?v=3D936QjnBgc&t=3s.

Revolution of the Heart: The Dorothy Day Story (57 minutes), a documentary on Dorothy Day, cofounder of the Catholic Worker Movement. Produced by Martin Doblmeier, Journey Films, 2020. http://journeyfilms.com/day/.